# TELL ME WHAT ?

GOLDEN MINDS PUBLISHING HOUSE

# TELL ME WHAT

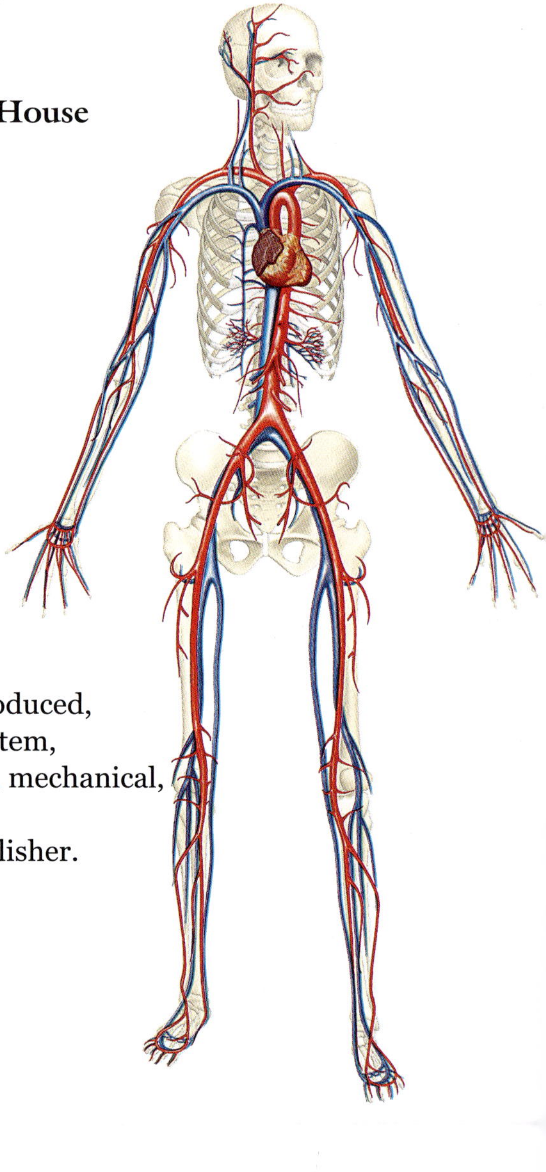



ISBN 978-81-8341-480-7

Published by:
Golden Minds Publishing House
326-330, Vardhaman Chambers,
Cawasji Patel Road, Kala Ghoda,
Fort, Mumbai - 400 001
Tel: 022 22821704 / 1705
email: goldenminds99@gmail.com



Printed in India.

# CONTENTS

# CONTENTS

# WHAT ARE TEETH MADE UP OF?

Teeth are calcified bone-like structures situated in both the jaws. A human develops two sets of teeth in his/her lifetime – baby teeth and permanent teeth. A tooth consists of four kinds of tissues – pulp, dentine, enamel and cementum. The pulp is the innermost layer of a tooth. It consists of connective tissues, blood, vessels and nerves. The blood vessels nourish the tooth. The hard, yellow substance which surrounds the pulp is the dentine which makes up the main part of the tooth. It is made up of mineral salts, water and living cells and is harder than bone. Above the dentine, is the enamel which is known as the crown of the tooth and is above the gum-line. The enamel is the hardest substance in the body. The cementum overlays the dentine in the root of the tooth. It is a hard bony substance which is surrounded by a periodontal ligament which contains the fibres that anchor the tooth in the bone of the gum.

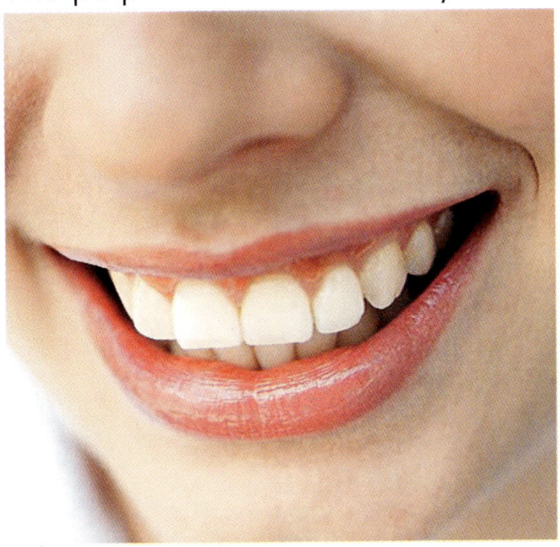

### BITS OF FACT

Although a tooth looks like a solid piece of bone, it contains a network of nerves, veins and arteries which enter the tooth through the root canal.

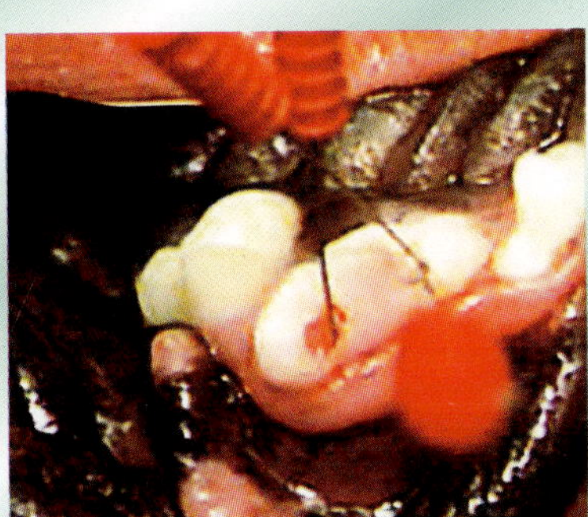

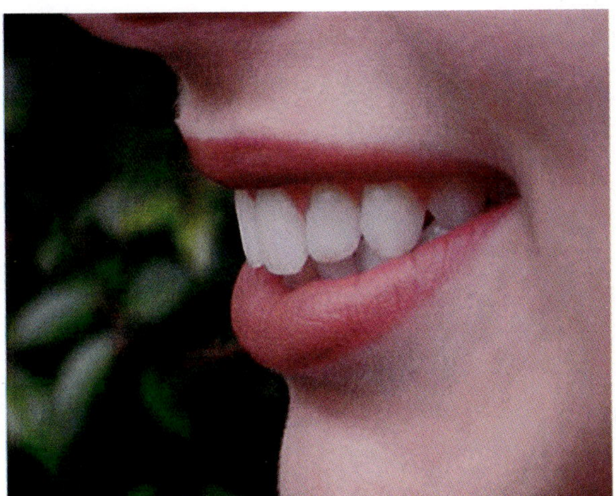

# WHAT ARE THE DIFFERENT TYPES OF TEETH?



Human beings develop two sets of teeth in their lifetime. The first set of 20 teeth are called the milk teeth or primary teeth. A baby is born with the teeth already developing in the jaws. The average age for the appearance of the first four front teeth is 7 months. The secondary or permanent set contains 32 teeth which begin to replace the first set around the age of 7 years. There are 16 teeth in each jaw. There are different types of teeth having different shapes to carry out various jobs. The incisors, which are flat and have sharp edges for biting, are at the front of the mouth. Next to them are the canines which have sharp points to tear the food. At the back of the mouth are the molars and the premolars which only appear in the second set of teeth. These are flattened and are used to grind the food into small pieces ready for swallowing. Molars, also called wisdom teeth, develop usually in late adolescence.

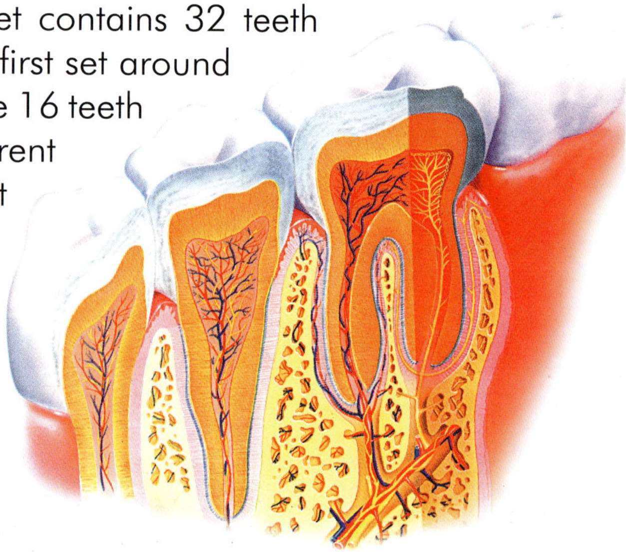

**BITS OF FACT**

The only bone in a human body not connected to another is the hyoid, a V-shaped bone located at the base of the tongue between the mandible and the voice box. Its function is to support the tongue and its muscles.

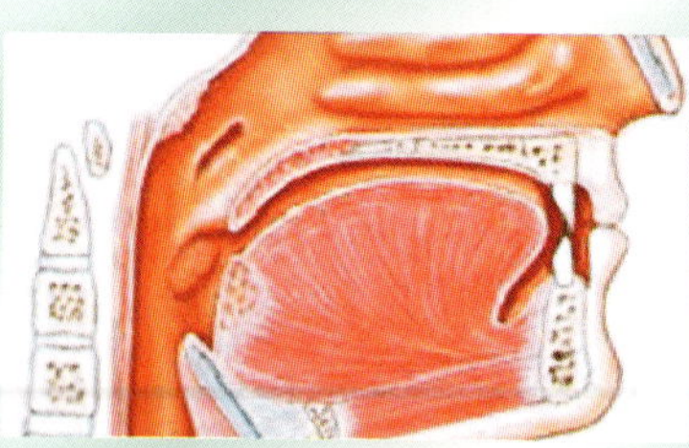

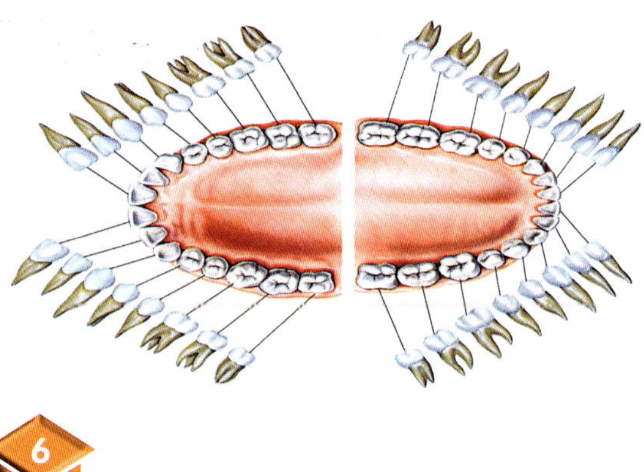

# WHAT ARE THE JUGULAR VEINS?

The jugular veins are in the neck and drain blood from the head, brain, face and neck and convey it towards the heart. There are four jugular veins, two on each side of the neck, namely external and internal jugulars. The external jugulars lie close to the surface and transport blood from the outer parts of the head and neck to the heart. They lie outside the sterno-cleidomastoid muscle, pass down the neck and join the subclavian vein. The internal jugulars lie deep inside and carry blood from the interior of the skull and the deeper tissues of the neck. They run down the inside of the neck outside the internal and common carotid arteries and unite with the subclavian vein to form the innominate vein.The external jugulars are much smaller as compared to the internal jugulars. Damaging a jugular vein may lead to rapid loss of blood and death if the wound is not attended immediately.

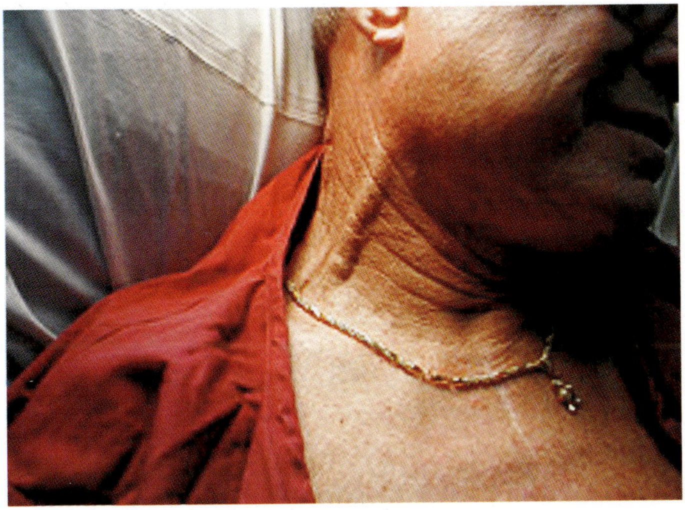

**BITS OF FACT**

Except for the pulmonary vein, which carries oxygenated blood from the lungs to the heart, veins carry deoxygenated blood.

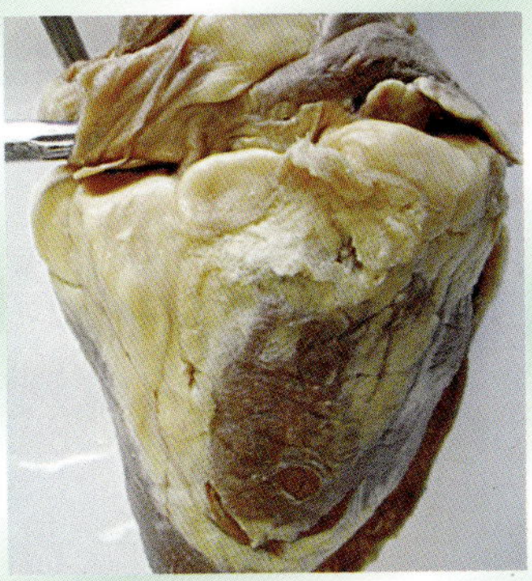

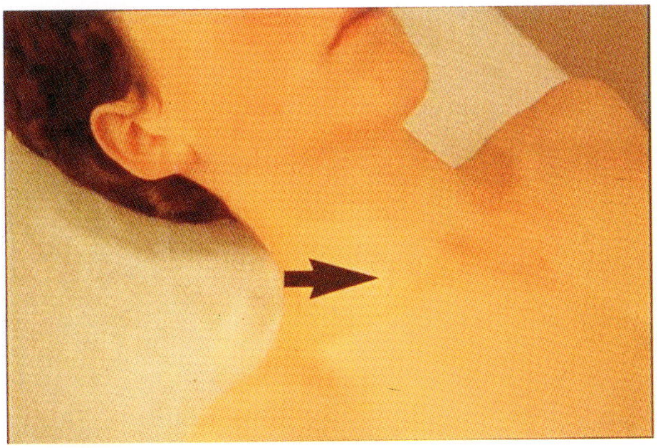

# What is the function of the spine?



The spine or vertebral column begins from the base of the skull and ends at the pelvis. It goes along the midline at the back. The vertebral column is not straight, but curved into an S-shape when viewed from the side. The spine is divided into five regions. It forms the central axis of the skeleton. The vertebral column is composed of vertebrae, discs, ligaments and muscles. The function of the spine is to provide both mobility and stability to the body. The muscles and ligamentous supporting structures of the spine enable the spine to function in an upright position, and also allow greater degrees of motion to permit the head and trunk to assume a variety of positions for various activities. Another function of the spine is to protect the spinal cord, a nervous structure which is located in a hollow canal running down the centre of the vertebral column. The spine is able to do all these functions because of its curved, segmented structure which is made up of 33 bones or vertebrae. These 33 vertebrae are separated from one another by pads of cartilage.

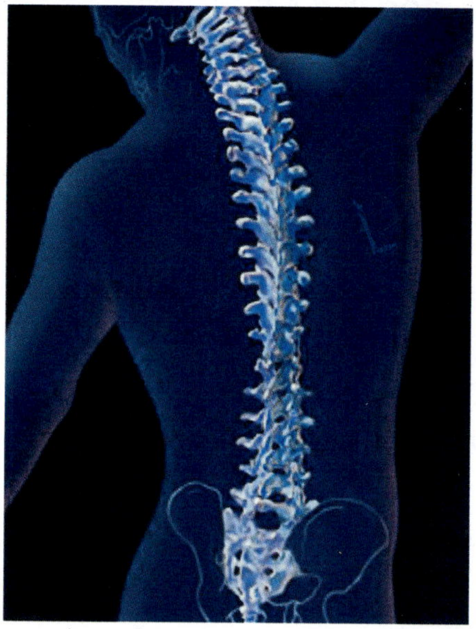

**BITS OF FACT**

Between the ages of 50 and 55, humans experience a distinct loss in height as discs between the vertebrae compress and shrink.

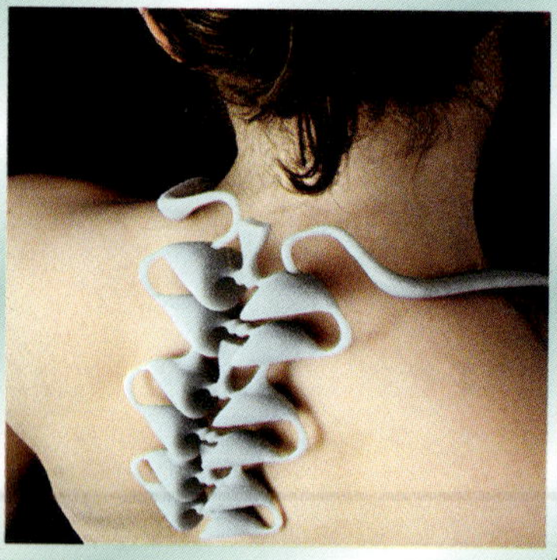

# WHAT GIVES THE RED COLOUR TO BLOOD?

Blood is a suspension of red and white blood cells, platelets, proteins and chemicals in a yellow-coloured fluid called plasma. Blood transports oxygen and other essential nutrients from the lungs and

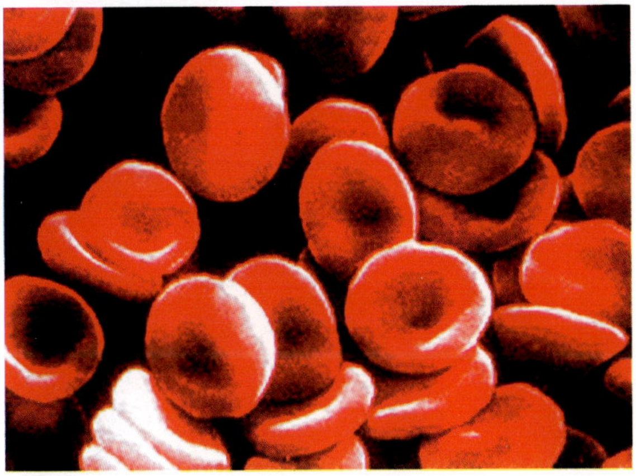

digestive tract to all parts of the body. Red blood cells are red only because they contain a protein-chemical called hemoglobin which is bright red in colour. Hemoglobin contains the element iron, making it an excellent vehicle for transporting oxygen and carbon dioxide. As blood passes through the lungs, oxygen molecules attach to the hemoglobin. As blood passes through the tissue of the body, the hemoglobin releases the oxygen to the cells. The empty hemoglobin molecules, then, bond with the carbon dioxide of the tissue or other waste gas, transporting it away. The life of blood cells is just for about four months. Afterwards, they start to break up. New red cells are immediately formed to replace the worn-out cells.

### BITS OF FACT

A normal human being has about 5 litres of blood. Each cubic milimetre of blood contains between four to six million red blood cells.

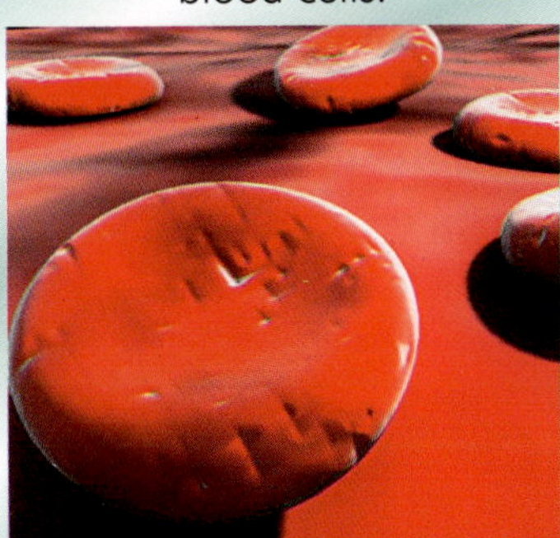

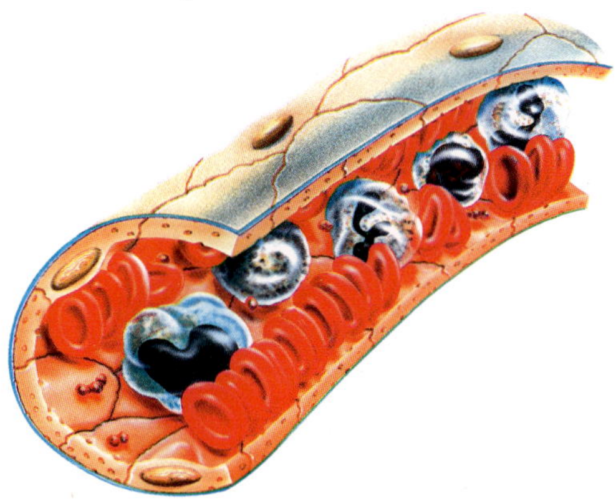

# WHAT HAPPENS WHEN WE BREATHE?

Breathing is a means by which a person absorbs oxygen from the surrounding atmosphere and exhales carbon dioxide from the blood stream through the lungs into the air. When a person breathes in, the intercostal muscles move his/her ribs upwards and downwards and the diaphragm pushes downwards. The diaphragm is a muscular layer which separates the chest-cavity from the abdominal cavity. It is attached at the back to the spine and to the ribs along the side of the chest. When the diaphragm is pushed downwards, air is drawn into the lungs. To reach the lungs, air flows through the mouth or nose, then through the trachea or the windpipe which is a tube beginning at the lower end of the voice box. From the trachea, the air passes into other tubes called the bronchi, which lead into the lungs.

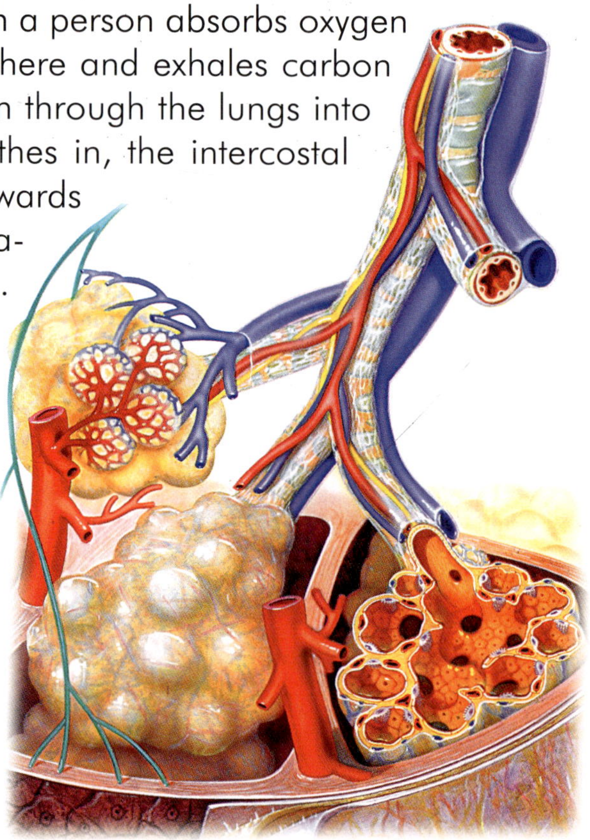

**BITS OF FACT**

An average person breathes 10 to 15 times a minute. But in times of stress or exercise, the demand for oxygen increases and thus breathing becomes faster.

# WHAT IS MEANT BY THE BRONCHIAL TREE?

The trachea or the windpipe branches at its lower end into two large air tubes called the bronchus. The right primary bronchus leads into the right lung and the left primary bronchus leads into the left lung. The outer wall of each bronchus is supported by cartilage. At the inside, the bronchus is lined with mucous membrane and many microscopic hair-like projections called cilia. These hair-like projections shift the trapped dust particles upwards. The primary bronchus, then, branch into smaller or

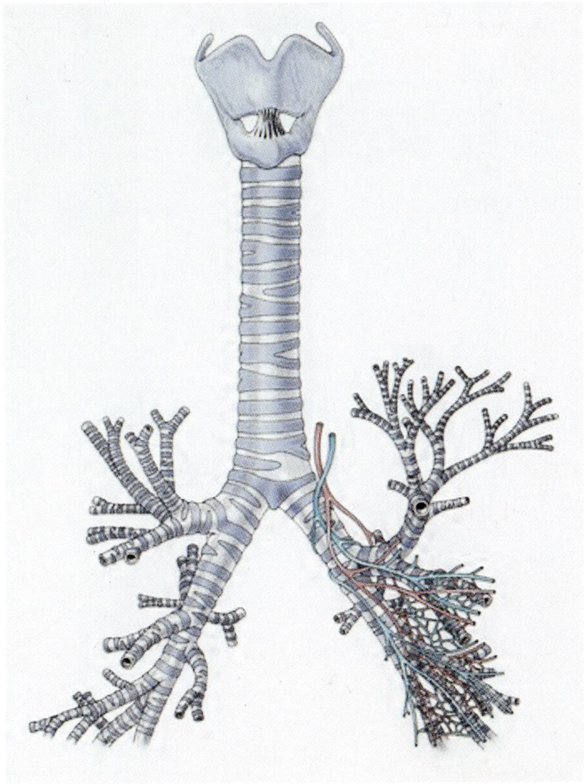

secondary bronchi at the entrance of the lung. There are three bronchi entering the right lung and two in the left. Each secondary bronchus divides into smaller bronchi. These further divide into hair-like terminal bronchioles which end at microscopic bubbles known as alveoli, the place where exchange of gases takes place. All these branching air-passages are referred to as the bronchial tree.

## BITS OF FACT

Close behind the windpipe is another long tube referred to as the esophagus, that provides passage for food and drink to the stomach.

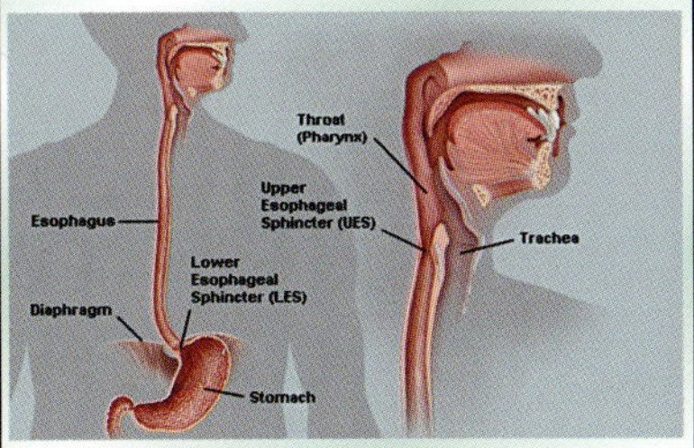

# WHAT IS THE BONE MADE UP OF?



A bone is the rigid, calcified tissue which makes up the body. Bones support the body and provide an attachment for the muscles. An adult bone consists of densely packed rod-shaped units called osteons. This composition is also called the Haversian system, as all these units are aligned in the same way. A bone is made up of different layers. The

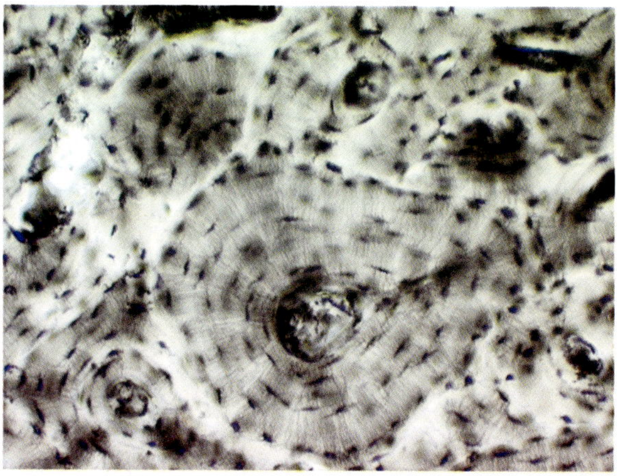

outermost layer is the periosteum, which is a thin fibrous membrane. This membrane covers the surface of the bone. Beneath this is the compact or cortical bone which surrounds the spongy bone. This bony tissue which looks like a sponge forms the bulk of the bone. It has gaps and spaces and is much lighter than the outer compact bone. These spaces are filled with blood vessels and jelly-like bone marrow. Blood cells are produced in this bone marrow. The major components of bone include the mineral salts, mainly calcium phosphate, which provides hardness and collagen fibres. These fibres provide strength.

**BITS OF FACT**

There is a very little difference between human skeleton bones and animal skeleton bones. Giraffes, well known for their long necks, have exactly the same number of neck bones as humans.

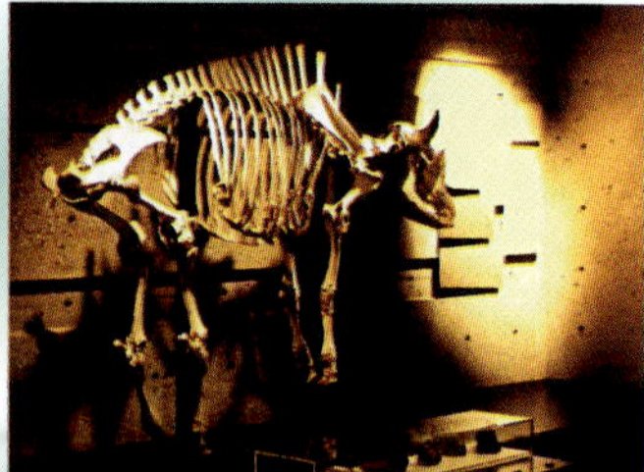

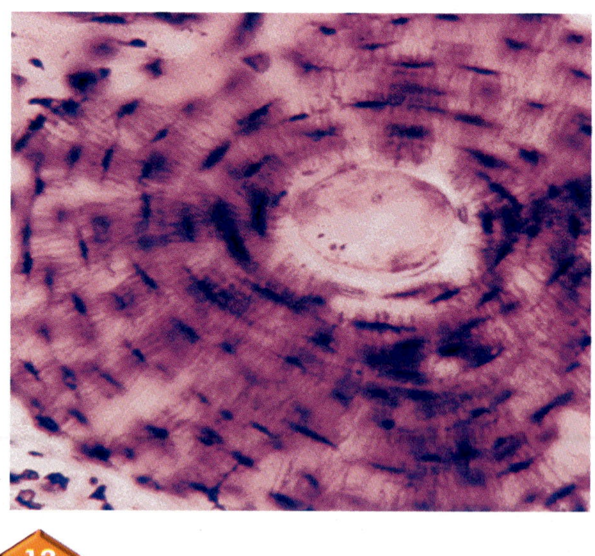

# WHAT DO YOU MEAN BY THE CONNECTIVE TISSUE?

The connective tissue is spread all over the body. The main function of the connective tissue is to bind, support and provide strength to other organs and tissues of the body. The connective tissue consists of cells

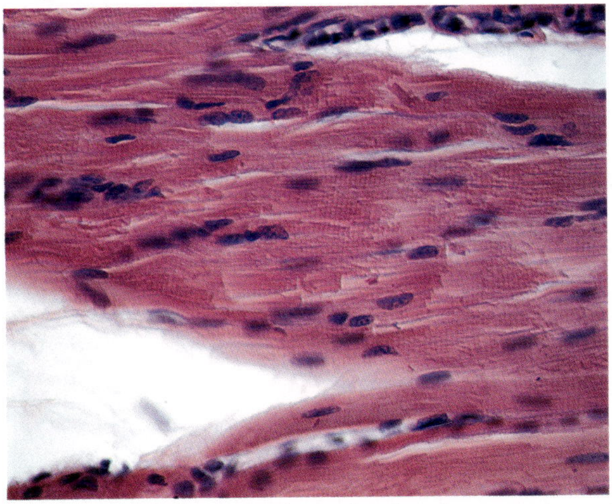

bound together and protein fibres in a medium called 'ground substance'. The ground substance can be fluid, gel or solid and is secreted by the cells of the connective tissue. The fibres provide support and strength along with flexibility. There are various forms of connective tissues, but all of them are made up of salts, water, protein and carbohydrates. Inside this jelly-like connective tissue are elastic threads to give elasticity, collagen to give strength, reticulin to give support, white cells and macrophages to fight infection, fat cells for storage and plasma cells to produce antibodies. There are five main types of connective tissues – loose connective tissue, dense connective tissue, cartilage, bone and blood.

**BITS OF FACT**

The first completely documented human tissue grafting was performed by a Swiss surgeon, Dr Jacques Reverdin.

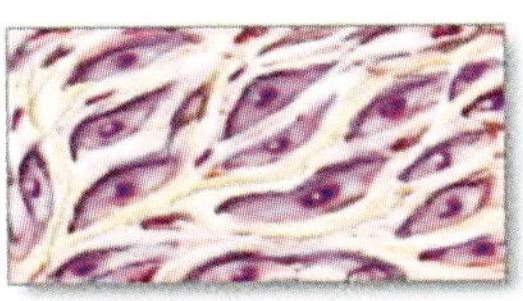

Connective tissue

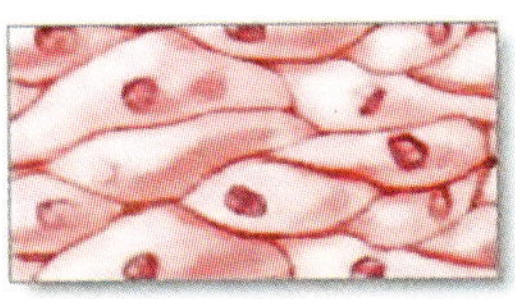

Epithelial tissue

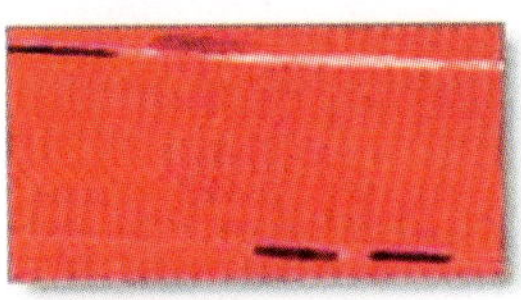

Muscle tissue

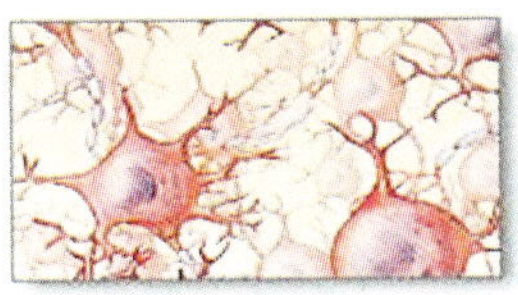

Nervous tissue

# What is a Human Body Made Up Of?

Cells are the basic structural units that make up all living organisms, be it plants, animals or human beings. Each person is made up of more than a million cells. The cell is the functional unit of all tissues and performs all the essential functions. Cells combine to make tissues and tissues into organs. The cells may be oval, spherical, flat or elongated in shape. Each cell is surrounded by a soft and elastic membrane known as plasma membrane. The cell membrane is filled with a semi transparent jelly-like fluid known as cytoplasm. This fluid contains important structural units called organelles. These organelles are concerned with the manufacture of protein, generation of energy, cell division and all other functions. The nucleus which contains genetic information in the form of DNA, controls all the functions of the cells.

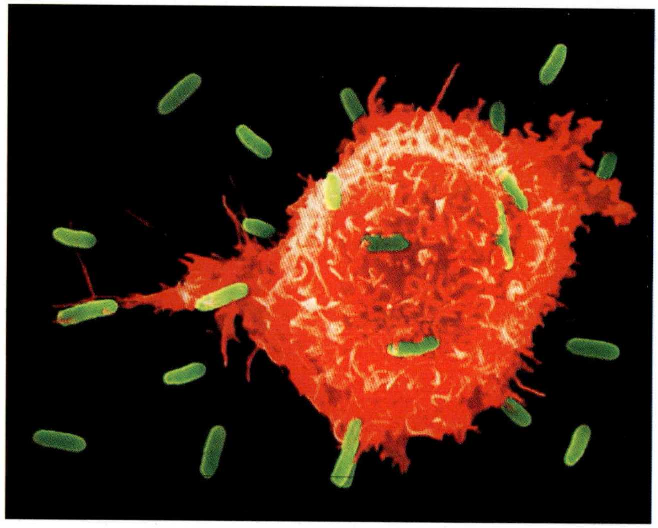

**BITS OF FACT**

The biggest cells are the nerve cells which may be about a metre long, but very fine. The tiniest cells are the red blood cells which are less than the thousandth of a centimetre across.

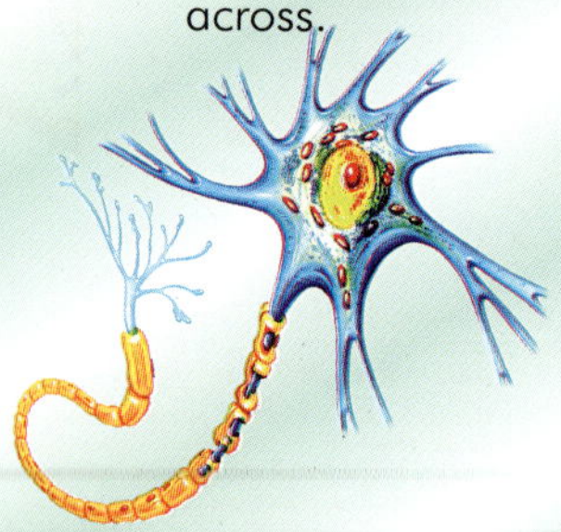

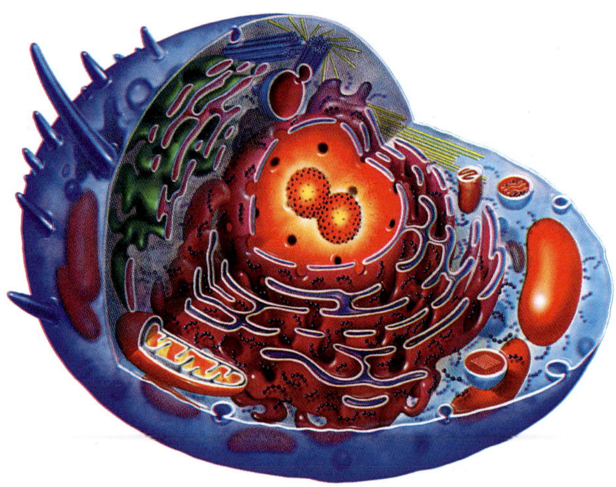

# What is the eye made up of?

The eye is a very complex and delicate structure through which we can see. The eye can be compared to a camera. It has an adjustable opening to let in the light. This opening is called the pupil. It has a lens which focuses light to form an image and the retina where the image is

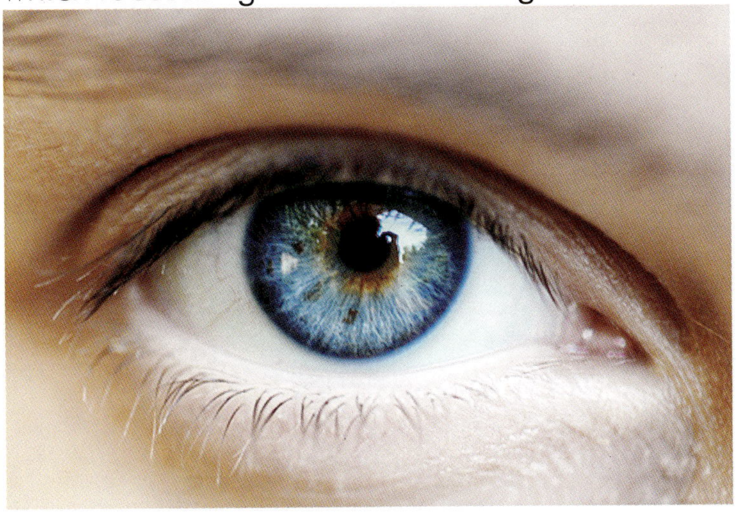

formed. Light enters the eye through the cornea, which is a transparent dome on the surface of the eye. Through the cornea, light enters the pupil of the eye. Light reaches the retina after passing through the optic lens and vitreous humour. The retina contains light sensitive cells called rods and cones, whose main function is to perceive light intensity. The retina has photoreceptors which send visual information to the brain. The optic nerve connects the eye to the brain.



**BITS OF FACT**

The eyes of the chameleon can move independently. Therefore, it can see in two different directions at the same time.

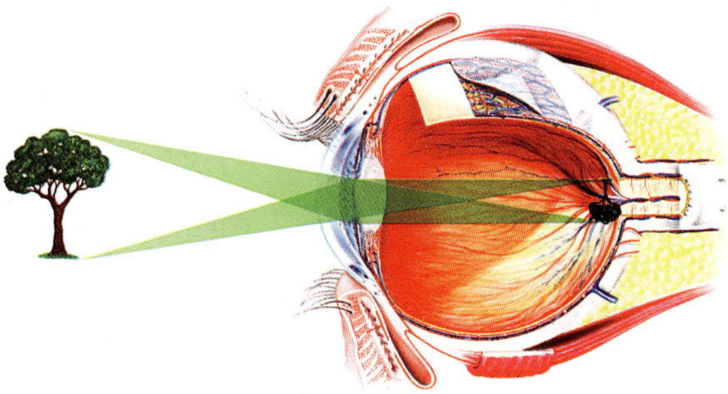

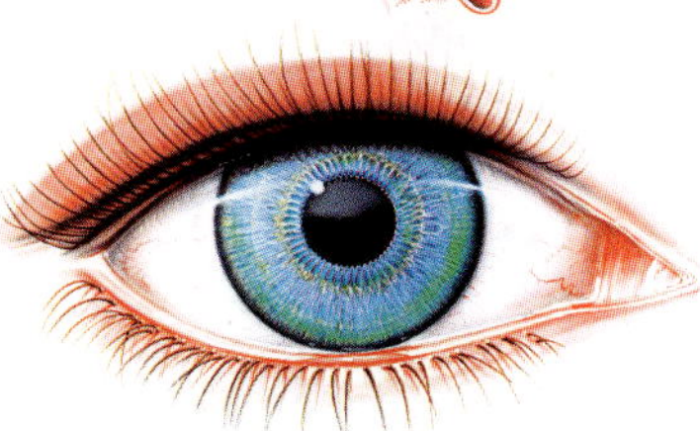

# What is the function of the kidneys?



There are two kidneys in a human body. They lie at the back, one on either side of the backbone. They look like reddish brown beans and are each about the size of a clenched fist. The nutrients and oxygen we take in is 'burned' to make energy for life to continue. This 'burning' process which takes place in our body cells also creates waste products which must be removed. The removal of waste products is termed as excretion and it is the kidneys which perform this function. Kidneys clean the blood by filtering out waste materials and straining off any water which the body does not require. Waste materials pass out through the water into the bladder, from where it is discharged from the body in the form of urine. Another function of the kidneys is to produce hormones which help regulate the blood pressure.

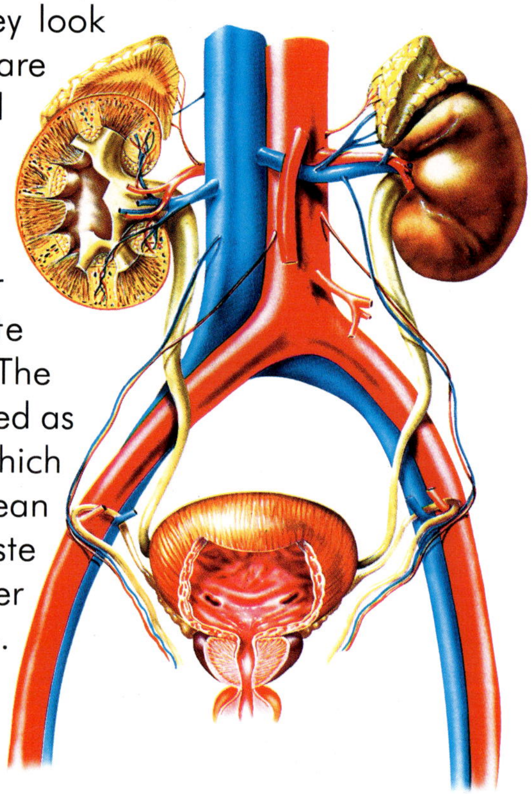

## BITS OF FACT

Approximately, 3 litres of water is lost from the body through breathing, sweating and in the form of urine every day. An adult produces about 1-1.5 litres of urine every day.

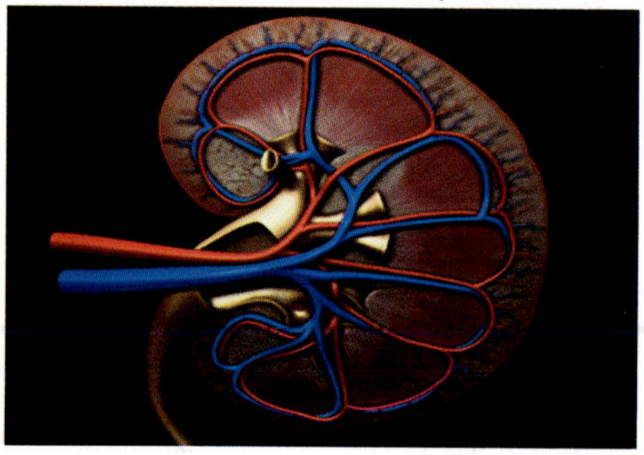

# What is the Function of the Retina?

The retina is the light sensitive layer at the rear inner surface of the eyeball. Light reaches the retina after passing through the cornea and the lens. When light reaches the retina, it is converted into nerve signals by specialized cells called photoreceptors. Based on their shape, they are classified into two types: rods and cones. Rod photoreceptors are more sensitive to light. These are connected together. Then, the sum of signals is sent to the brain. They are good for sensing brightness and movement rather than detailed vision. There are about 125 million rod cells. The cone receptors are not as sensitive to light as the rods, but they can detect colours. Cone cells are responsible for detailed vision. There are about 7 million cone cells.

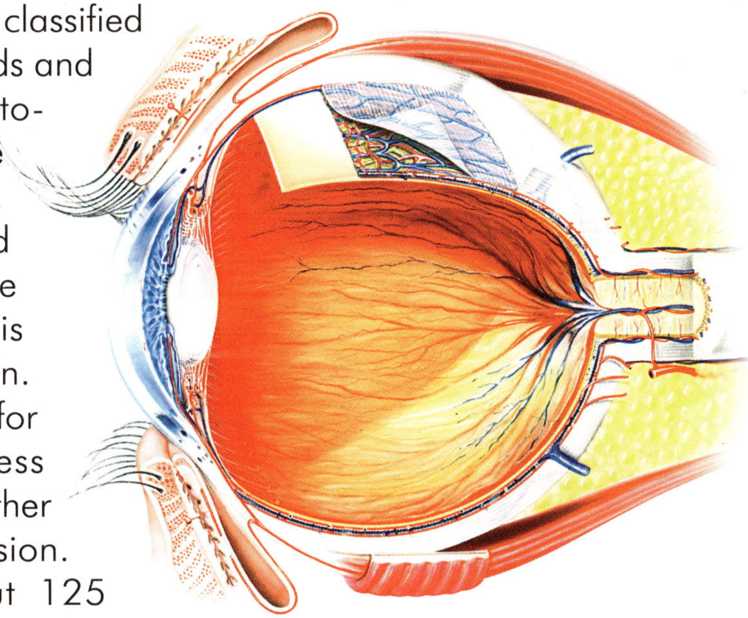

**BITS OF FACT**

Fish only have rods in the retina: 25 million rods/sq. mm. Perhaps, they need this high density of photoreceptors to detect the dim biolumninescence that exists in the ocean depths.

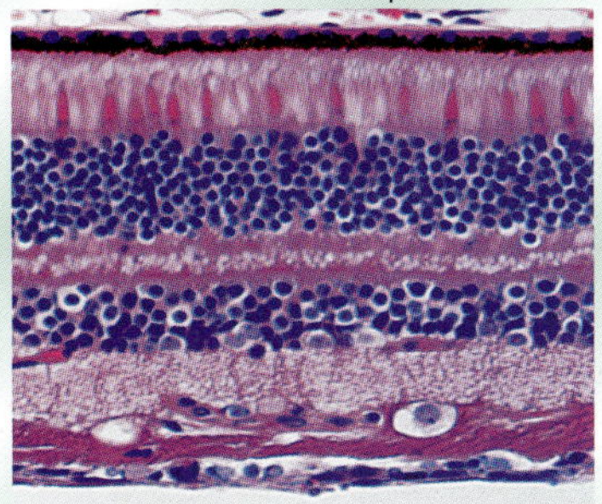

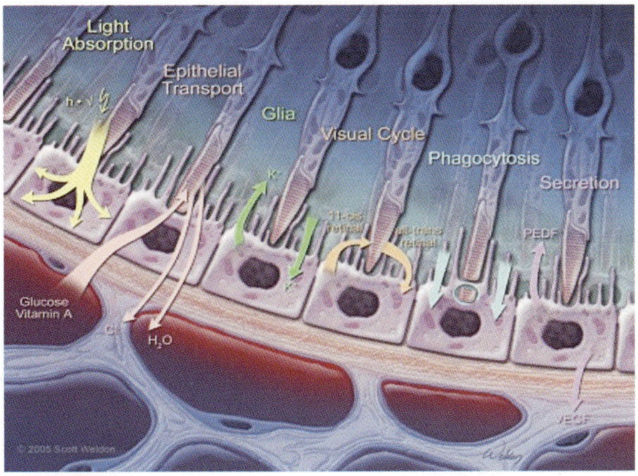

# What is the function of the heart?



The heart is a muscular organ which pumps blood around the body. It is made up of two halves separated by a thick muscular wall. Each half is further divided into an upper and a lower chamber. Thus, the heart has four chambers, namely a left and a right atrium and a left and a right ventricle. Blood rich in oxygen from the lungs flows into the left atrium and is forced through a valve into the left ventricle. From there, the blood is pumped out into the aorta which is the largest artery of the body. Finally, the blood goes to the rest of the body. Deoxygenated blood or blood carrying waste products from all over the body goes into the right atrium and then the right ventricle. From there, the blood is pumped towards the lungs for exchange of gases to take place. In the lungs, the blood gets rid of carbon dioxide and takes oxygen, ready to go back to the heart. Then, the same process is repeated.

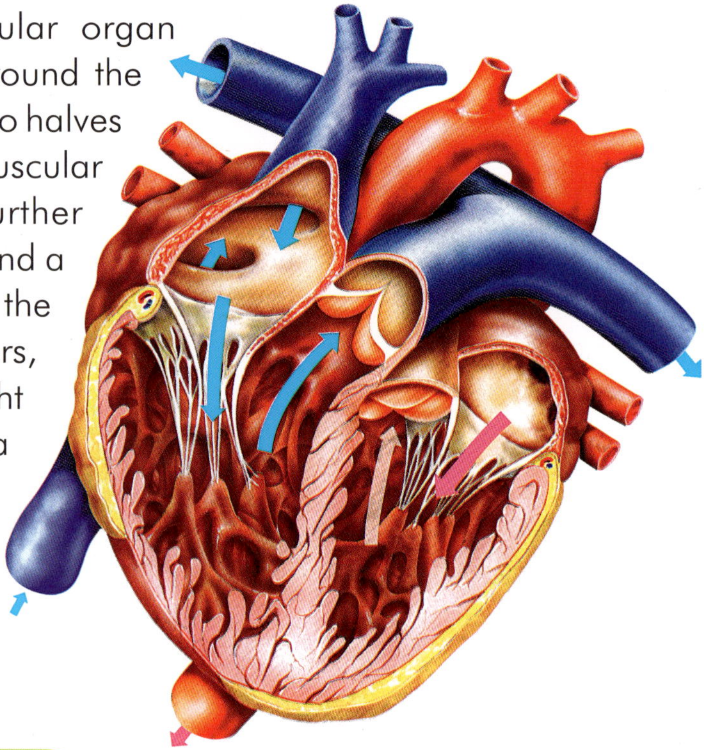

**BITS OF FACT**

The average weight of a heart in a man is 310 gm and in a woman 260 gm. The heart of an adult beats nearly 70 times a minute.

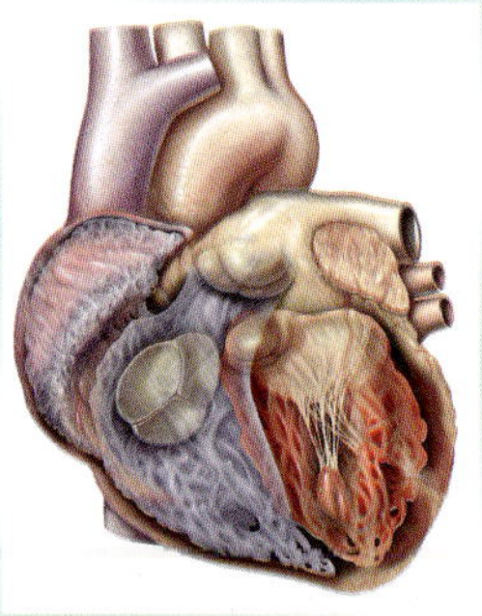

# WHAT IS THE IMMUNE SYSTEM?

The immune system is a complex network of organs, cells and proteins whose function is to protect the body from diseases. It is due to this system that we say that the body is capable of protecting itself from the invasion of disease-causing microbes. The immune system is scattered all over the body. White blood cells, called lymphocytes, are stored in the lymphatic or immune system of the body. This system is actually a network of thin tubes carrying a watery fluid called lymph. At the end of the lymph are small lumps, called lymph nodes, where lymphocytes are stored. Lymph nodes filter out and destroy foreign bodies before they get into circulation. They also activate the lymphocytes to produce certain antibodies, which protect and repair the damaged area.

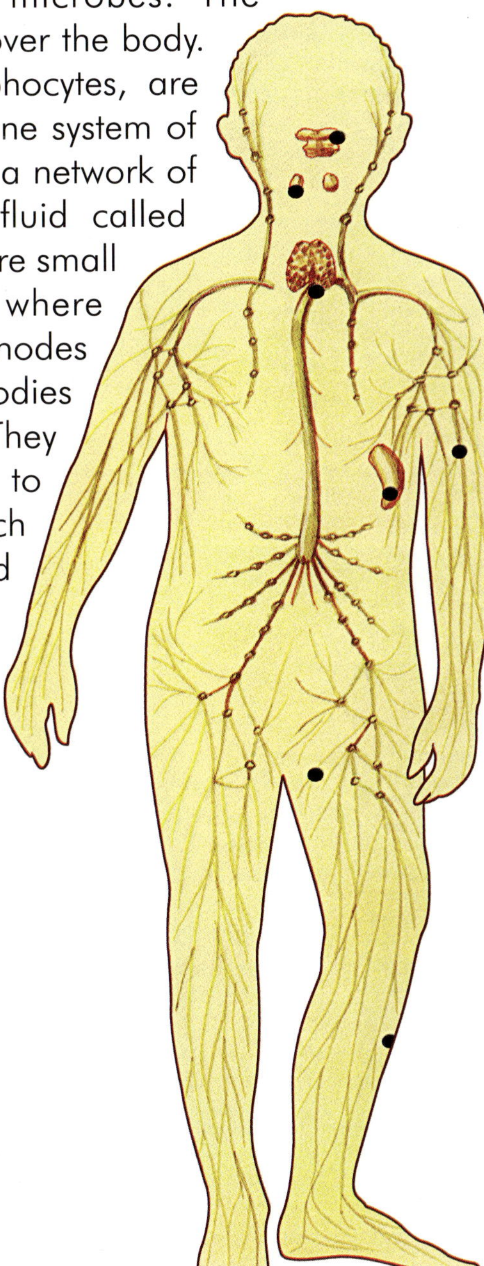

## BITS OF FACT

If a person has an adequate sleep or rest, balanced diet and appropriate exercise, his/her body will produce over one billion immune cells within 24 hours to strengthen the immune system.

# What is the skin made up of?

The skin is the outer waterproof covering of the body. The skin protects the body from external agents, extremes of temperature, viruses, bacteria and parasites. It contains nerves which respond to pain, touch and temperature. The skin is made up of two layers, namely the outer layer called the epidermis and the inner layer called the dermis. The epidermis is the skin a person sees on his/her body. It is made of dead cells. The epidermis consists of five sub-layers. As cells in the top layer die, they are replaced by new cells from the lower layers. It takes about four weeks for cells, formed at the bottom layer, to reach and replace those in the top layer. The inner layer, the dermis, contains a network of blood vessels, nerves and fat lobules. The dermis is a network of protein fibres and elastin which provide strength and support to the skin.

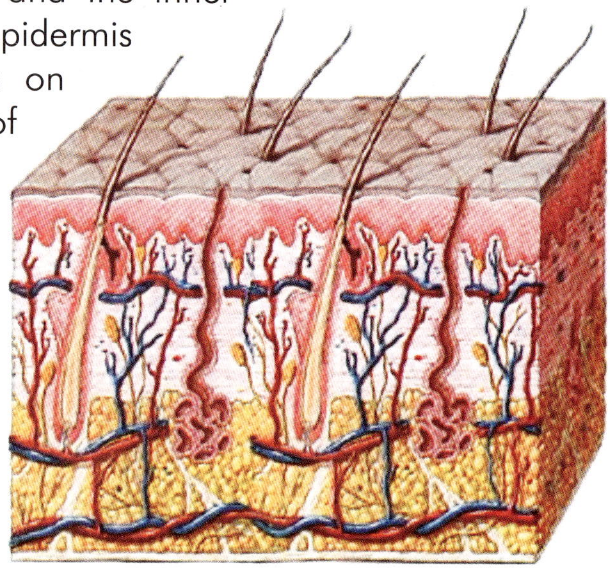



**BITS OF FACT**

The skin covers a surface area of 1.75 square metre. It varies in thickness from about 1 mm on the eyelids to about 5 mm at the bottom of the feet and on the palms.

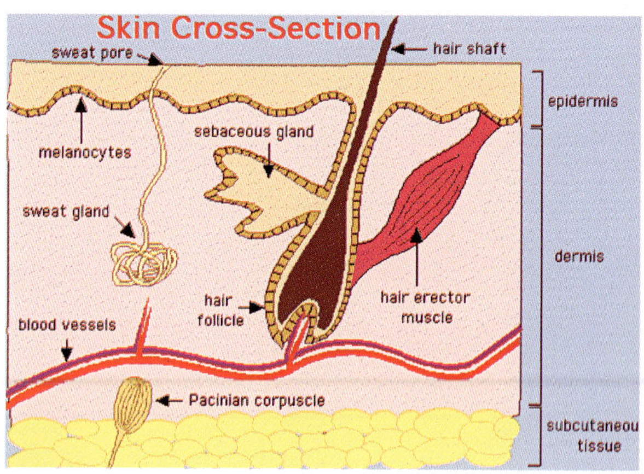

# WHAT IS THE FUNCTION OF THE ORGAN OF CORTI?



The ear is made up of three parts, namely the outer ear, the middle ear and the inner ear. The inner ear contains a structure called the cochlea, which is a small, spiral-shaped structure. It contains fluid and special hair that serve as sound sensors. The vibrations of the membrane covering the oval window cause waves to form in the cochlear fluid. These vibrations are picked up by the organ of Corti, which is the hearing organ situated in the cochlea. The organ of corti consists of the rows of cells with fine hair-like projections under a layer of membrane. The movement of the hair provides the brain with information on the volume or intensity of sound. Soft sounds stimulate only a few cells, whereas loud sounds stimulate many cells. When vibrations in the fluid reach them, the nerve endings fire off electrical impulses which are sent along the nerve to the brain to be interpreted as sounds.

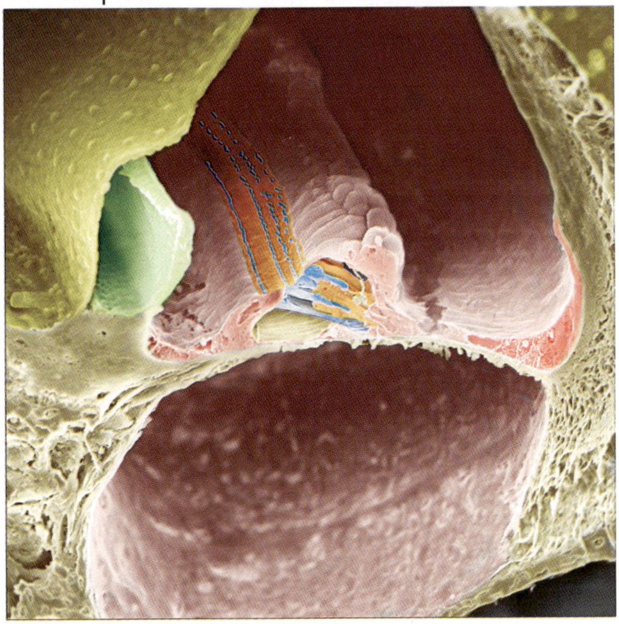

## BITS OF FACT

Elephants have a hearing range between 1 and 20,000 Hz. The very low frequency sounds are in the "infrasound" range. Humans cannot hear sounds in the infrasound range.

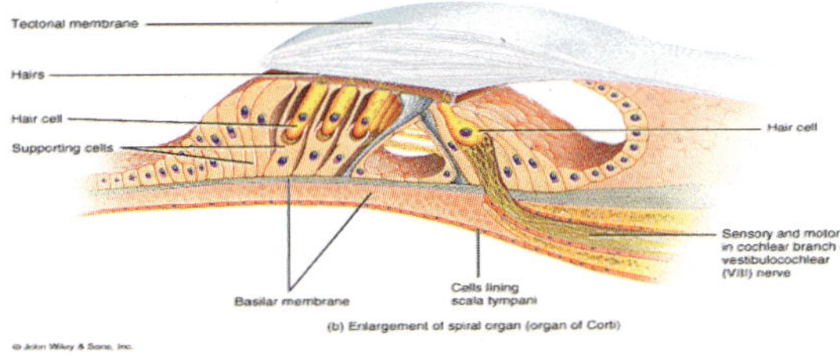


(b) Enlargement of spiral organ (organ of Corti)

# What is a tendon?



A tendon is a glistening white cord of the connective tissue that attaches a muscle to a bone. It is similar in structure to a ligament, which connects a bone to a bone. The tendons play a very crucial role in the movement of the human body by transmitting the force created by muscles to move bones. In this way, they allow muscles to control movement from a distance. Tendons are tough, fibrous and flexible. They are, however, not elastic. Tendons are made up of collagen fibres, ground substances and cells, which are referred to as fibrocytes in t endons. At the point where a tendon touches a bone, the tendon fibres gradually pass into the substance of the bone and meld with it. Some tendons run inside a fibrous sheath. Between the sheath and the tendon is a thin film of lubricant called synovial fluid. This helps tendons to glide smoothly over the surrounding parts.

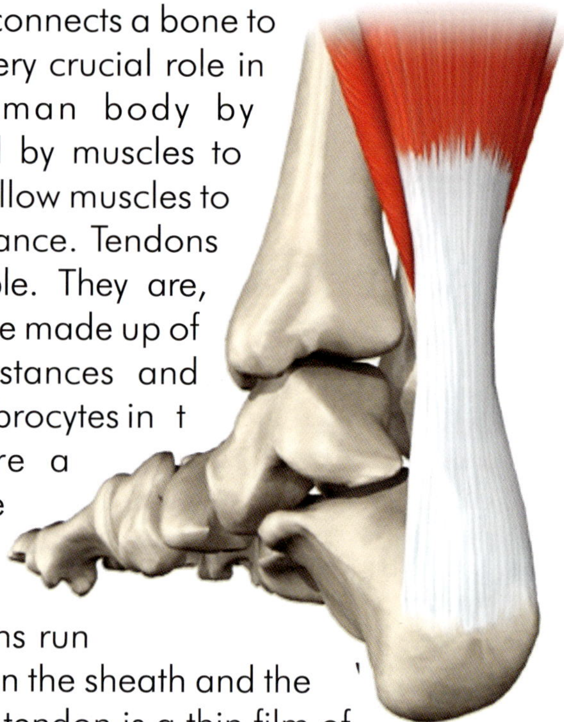

## BITS OF FACT

In the hand, tendons link the fingers with the forearm muscles allowing a full range of movement. In the foot, the calf muscle is connected to the heel bone by the Achilles tendon.

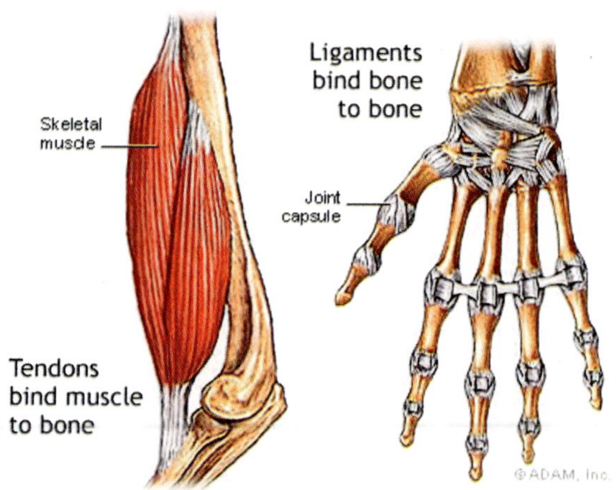

# WHAT DO YOU MEAN BY MARSUPIALS?

Marsupials are animals whose babies are born before they are ready to survive in the outside world. The newborn undergoes most of its development attached to the mother's nipples and nourished by her milk. The young ones develop in the mother's pouch. There are about 270 species of marsupials which include kangaroos, koalas and opossums. Kangaroos are the largest marsupials. The female kangaroo has a pouch in her belly to protect her young ones. Inside the pouch, the baby sucks on its mother's teats. When the baby kangaroo is born, it is naked and looks like a tiny jelly baby and is a few centimetres long with two tiny arms. Soon, the baby moves itself up through the fur on its mother's belly and into her pouch. The baby kangaroo lives here and grows for 6-8 months sucking on its mother's teats. Koalas are also marsupials which look like teddy bears. A koala baby spends 6 months in its mother's pouch and another 6 months riding on her back.

**BITS OF FACT**

Marsupials have short gestation (period from mating to birth) period. The shortest gestation period is that of the opossum. Its babies develop in 12-13 days. The longest marsupial gestation period is of the grey kangaroo. Its babies develop in 37 days.

# WHAT DO YOU MEAN BY REPTILES?

Reptiles are vertebrates (animals with backbones) and are usually covered with scales or plates which form armours. Reptiles are cold blooded, which means that their body temperatures depend on their surroundings. For example, in cold weather it feels cold. Most reptiles lay eggs, except for some lizards and snakes which give birth to young ones. Reptiles are found in various parts of the world. Since they are cold blooded, many of them cannot survive in very cold places like the polar regions. Reptiles include crocodiles, alligators, snakes, lizards, tortoises and turtles. There are 22 species of crocodiles. They are armourplated, have powerful tails and deadly fangs. They are very good swimmers and can move very fast in water. The bodies of snakes are covered with waterproof scales. They are devoid of eyelids and legs. Tortoises and turtles have leathery skins and shells to protect their bodies.

**BITS OF FACT**

The South American snake, the anaconda, is the largest reptile with a length of over 9 metres. The reptile which is mostly eaten by human beings is the green turtle.

# WHAT IS A LEMUR?

The lemur belongs to the most primitive members of the order Primates which comprise monkeys. Lemurs are small furry creatures with long tails and big eyes. Lemurs are found on the islands of Madagascar, Africa and some areas of Asia. Most lemurs live on trees except the ring-tailed lemur which lives mostly on the ground. These ring-tailed lemurs get their name from their black ringed tails. Lemurs feed on a mixed diet which consists of fruits, seeds, insects and small birds. Most lemurs are active at night, but some like the ring-tailed are active during the day. One large lemur lives in Madagascar which is popularly known as "Sifaca". It is brightly coloured white with black, red or brown markings. There is a fold of skin between its arm and body which helps in its long jumps from one tree to another. Lemurs use their sense of smell to communicate with one another. These primates have scent glands on their bottoms and on their feet that leave odours on surfaces they cross.

## BITS OF FACT

The smallest of all the lemurs is 13 centimetres in length and has a tail of 15 centimetres. It is popularly known as the "mouse lemur". This little animal stores fat around the base of the tail in favourable times.

# WHAT IS THE PURPOSE OF AN ELEPHANT'S TRUNK?



The African elephant is the largest land animal, growing as tall as 4 metres and weighing more than 6,000 kg. The trunk of the elephant is the most outstanding part of the elephant's body. It is an extension of the nose and the upper lip. The trunk is very powerful and flexible. The elephant uses its long trunk to breathe, to smell and to gather food. It is very good for holding on to things and it is so sensitive that it can even pick up very small objects. The trunk is also used for drawing up water. The water is then transferred to the elephant's mouth for drinking. The trunk is also used to draw up water which the elephant, then, showers all over its body. The elephant also enjoys dust baths, using the trunk to gather the dust and blow it over itself. In this way, it gets rid of flies and ticks. The trunk is also used to warn the other elephants of danger, by giving a loud blast, called a trumpet.

**BITS OF FACT**

The elephant's trunk contains over 4,00,000 muscles. An adult elephant can hold 4.5 litres of water in its trunk. On an average, it needs about 20 trunkfuls of water in a day.

# WHAT IS THE DIFFERENCE BETWEEN THE INDIAN AND AFRICAN ELEPHANTS?

The main difference between the Indian and African elephants is that the African elephant is much larger than the Indian elephant. An elephant uses its large ears to flap them and keep them cool. African elephants have larger ears than the Indian elephants. An elephant has a lip at the end of the trunk. An Indian elephant has just one lip, whereas an African elephant has two lips. There is also a little difference in the feet of two species. There are five digits on the front feet of the Indian elephant, while the African elephant has four. The tusks of an elephant are actually enlarged incisor teeth. They are used for digging up roots, boring for water and for fighting. Only the males of the Indian elephants have tusks. In case of the African elephants, both male and female have tusks. Also, the tusks of the Indian elephant are smaller. An African elephant does not live for more than 50 years, whereas an Indian elephant lives for an average of 70 years.

## BITS OF FACT

The tusks of the male African elephant can grow up to 3.5 m long each and may weigh up to 109 kg each. The tusks of the extinct woolly mammoth were up to 5 metres long each.

# WHAT DO BROWN BEARS LOVE TO EAT?

There are seven species of bears. The Alaskan brown bear, which is also known as the Kodiak bear, is the largest of all. Other brown bears are found in North America. The polar bear is the only bear to live in the Arctic region. The polar bear feeds only on fish, seals and walruses. The number of brown bears in Europe and Asia is now quite low. Brown bears eat just about anything they can find. Their diet, like most bears, changes according to the seasons. Vegetable matter, such as roots, tubers, grasses, herbaceous plants, corns, berries, fruits, and nuts comprise 60 - 90 % of their diet. Common animal matter consumed are insects, rodents, hoofed mammals, fish and carcasses of dead sea mammals. The brown bear loves to eat honey. Without bothering about the stinging bees, the brown bear will open a wild beehive. After eating, it will roll on the ground or rub itself against a tree to remove the bees that have stuck onto its fur. It also goes into the river to catch fish.

**BITS OF FACT**

The only bear which lives in South America is the spectacled bear. It gets its name because it has white rings around its eyes which look like spectacles. Actually, this bear has very weak eyesight compared to other bears.

# WHAT DO YOU MEAN BY CAMOUFLAGE?

Camouflage is a way in which an animal's colour or shape matches its surroundings. In other words, it is an animal's ability to hide itself from its predator and prey. Animals have many ways of camouflaging themselves in order to hide themselves from their enemies. Paradoxophyla palmata, a narrow-headed frog native to Madagascar, is a leading example. The frog's brown and yellow colouring, as well as its rough texture, allows it to blend in with the mud and tree trunks in its environment. The spots on the leopard and the stripes of the tiger are so well camouflaged, that it is difficult to make out whether they are or not, until they move. In order to match with the surrounding, the chameleon can change its colour. Similarly, the praying mantis of Malaysia can change its colour and look like a flower. The sloth of the South American jungles has an unusual way of camouflage. It has coarse hair which is grooved. Within these grooves grow simple, green algae. This gives a green appearance and helps the sloth to conceal itself from predators.

### BITS OF FACT

The shingleback lizard has a short plump tail, which looks like the head. As the creature seems to have two heads, the predator does not know which end to attack.

# WHAT IS THE DANGER FACED BY APES AND MONKEYS?

Many apes and monkeys are in danger of extinction, because of the rapid destruction of the rain-forests. Habitat loss due to the clearing of tropical forests for agriculture, logging and for the collection of fuel wood are some of the reasons responsible for the declining number of primates. In addition, climate change is altering the habitats of many species. The mountain gorilla of Africa, the orangutan of Asia and numerous monkeys of South America are among the few. The baby orangutans are very popular pets. In order to capture the babies, hunters kill their mothers first. In this way, the babies become weak and they are easy to catch. The captured babies may die of diseases because animals are likely to catch human diseases. Together with this, their habitat is also being destroyed, which results in the decreasing number of orangutans. Similarly, the snow monkey of China is also hunted for its beautiful hair.

## BITS OF FACT

The cololris monkey of Africa has long, silky fur which hangs down from its side. Because of its magnificent fur, it has been killed in thousands.

# What do giant pandas eat?

Pandas are black, large furry mammals that live in the bamboo forest of western China and Tibet. Their main food are bamboo shoots and leaves. An adult panda can eat up to 30-40 kg of bamboo each day.

Giant pandas are among the rarest species of animals in the world. A giant panda's digestive system is more similar to that of a carnivore than a herbivore. So much of what is eaten is passed as waste. To make up for the inefficient digestion, a panda needs to consume a comparatively large amount of food from 20 to 40 pounds of bamboo each day to get all its nutrients. To obtain this much food means that a panda must spend 10 to 16 hours a day eating. The rest of its time is spent mostly sleeping and resting. The balance consists of other grasses and occasional small rodents or the fawns of musk deer. In zoos, giant pandas eat bamboos, sugar canes, rice gruel (a special high-fibre biscuit), carrots, apples and sweet potatoes.

## BITS OF FACT

A newborn cub weighs three to five ounces and is about the size of the stick of butter. Pink, hairless, and blind, the cub is 1/900th the size of its mother.

# WHAT DO POLAR BEARS EAT?

The polar bear is found in the Arctic Circle. It is able to survive the severe cold because it's body is well insulated with the fur and the fat. It can swim for over 150 km. A healthy diet for a polar bear consists of about 2kg (4.4lbs) of fat per day. Ringed seals, with their high fat-content, are the polar bear's primary prey. Polar bears mostly eat seals which are found beneath the ice. The seals make holes in the ice so that they may come up to breathe in air. The polar bears can sniff these holes. They wait until the seals come out from the holes to breathe.

As soon as the seals pop up, the bears attack them with their paws and the seals are killed. Polar bears also eat grass, fish and berries during the summer months. A polar bear gives birth to its young ones in a den which is dug in the snow. The young ones stay in the den for about three months. At the time of birth, their weight is less than 1 kg each. By the time they come out of the den, they are 10 kg.

**BITS OF FACT**

The average adult male bear is 2.5 metres long and its weight is 408 kg which is amazingly equal to that of five adult people.

# What is the purpose of the flat nose of the pig?

There are many different kinds of pigs reared around the world. A pig has four toes on each foot. Each toe ends in a hoof. The two middle hooves are divided in all pigs, except the mule foot breed which has a solid or single toed hoof in the middle of each foot. A pig has a large head with a long snout which is strengthened by a special bone called the prenasal bone and by a disc of cartilage in the tip. The snout is used to dig into the soil to find food and is a very sensitive sense-organ. That is why the pig has an excellent sense of smell. The shape of the nose helps it to turn over the soil and sniffs out roots, insects, larvae and other food. In France, pigs are used to find truffles, a type of fungus which grows underground. Female pigs are chosen because truffles smell like male pigs and the female pigs are, hence, attracted towards them. Pigs reproduce very rapidly. Their gestation period lasts for 114 days, after which they give birth to 8-12 piglets at a time.

**BITS OF FACT**

A baby pig, or piglet, weighs about 1.5 kilograms at birth and will double its weight in just 7 days.

# What are sloths?



Sloths are strange-looking mammals found in Central and South America. They reside in trees and are never visible away from forest areas. There are two types of sloths, namely three-toed and two-toed sloths. A three-toed sloth has three-toes on each foot, whereas a two-toed sloth has two toes on its front feet and three on the back. Sloths are believed to be very lazy animals. They are the slowest land mammals. They move at the rate of 1.8-2.4 metres per minute. They spend about 18-20 hours a day sleeping. With the help of their strong, long claws they hang around the branches of trees. Their grip is so strong that even if they sleep in this manner they do not fall. They usually crawl about slowly at night in search of tree leaves and twigs. The fur of a sloth is grey and shabby. Sometimes algae grow in its fur which gives it a greenish shade. This actually helps the sloth because the green colour helps it stay unnoticed by predators like eagles, jaguars and other animals.

**BITS OF FACT**

The orangutan is the largest fruit-eating animal in the world and it rarely comes out of the trees in which it lives.

# What do farm animals give us?

Farm animals include cattle, sheep and hens. There are about 200 breeds of domestic cows. Dairy cows are female cows which are reared for milk, cheese and butter production. The female cows give birth to one calf each and after that, they give milk twice a day. A typical dairy cow provides 16 litres of milk daily, which sums to almost 6,000 litres each year. Male cows are reared mainly for their meat, which is called beef. Sheep, goats and ilama-like alpacas are all reared for their wool, which is used in making clothes. Hairy sheep are kept for their milk and meat whereas the woolly ones are kept for their wool. About 3.3 million alpacas are farmed for their long and fine wool which grows almost to the ground. Sheep were domesticated about 10,000 years ago. Today, there are more than 700 million sheep in the world and 800 different breeds. Hens are farmed for their eggs and meat. Hens lay one or two eggs a day. Every day, the eggs must be taken away from them so that they may not hatch.

## BITS OF FACT

Special breeds of hens lay about 300 eggs in a year. They incubate their eggs and raise young ones. A mother hen turns her eggs approximately 50 times a day.

# WHAT DOES THE DOG FAMILY CONSIST OF?

The dog family is a large group of four-legged, long-nosed, meat-eating animals. They include dogs, wolves, foxes, jackals and coyotes. All kinds of dogs have long, canine teeth which are used for piercing and tearing their prey. Dogs have a very good sense of smell and hearing. The largest among the wild dogs is the wolf. Wolves are very good at teamwork while attacking their prey bigger than themselves such as moose, deer, caribou and musk oxen. Usually, 7-20 wolves form a group known as a pack. They communicate with the other members of their group by howling. Foxes are cunning hunters which prowl in the night alone or in pairs. Their prey includes rats, mice and rabbits. Another fearsome hunter is the group of jackals which are found all over Asia and Africa. In addition to the hunted animals, they also eat the remains of the animals killed by big cats.

## BITS OF FACT

Coyotes may scan the sky for ravens flying in circles. Coyotes know that birds often hover over dead animals. So, finding the birds frequently leads to finding a free meal.

# What are the different types of animals based on food?

According to the eating habits, animals are divided into three categories, namely herbivorous, carnivorous and omnivorous. Herbivorous animals are those which usually eat only plants. Herbivores include animals like cattle, elephants and horses. They either eat grass or leaves, barks and buds of trees and bushes. They have tough, crowned teeth to eat the hard plant-food. Also, they are found eating most of the time. Carnivorous animals are those which eat only animal flesh. Carnivores have pointed canine teeth for piercing and tearing the meat. Carnivores include all dogs and big cats like lions, tigers, cheetahs etc. Carnivores eat only occasionally because meat is very nourishing. They tend to rest after each meal. Some carnivores like hyenas do not hunt. Instead, they feed on the remains of dead animals. Omnivorous animals are those which eat both plants and animals. Many primates such as monkeys, apes and humans are omnivores.

**BITS OF FACT**

Lions usually catch something to eat every four days. They can eat up to 40 kg of meat in a single meal. After which, they rest for 24 hours.

# What do hippopotamuses look like?

Hippopotamuses are, big, grey, pig-like creatures that live in Africa. The word, hippopotamus, comes from the ancient Greek word 'hippo' meaning horse and 'potamus' meaning river. Hippos spend their days moving about in rivers and swamps. They only come out at night to feed. Its eyes, nose and ears are situated on the top of its head. Hence, it remains above the water, even when the rest of the body is completely submerged. By spending the daytime in water, hippos avoid the heat of the Sun. The skin of the hippo loses water very easily in the hot, dry daytime, but the cool, moist night air suits it very well. Male hippos fight in order to defend a territory or the right to mate with the females of that territory. First, they threaten one another by grunting, scattering dung with their tails. Then, they show off their large canine teeth or 'tusks'.

## BITS OF FACT

The mouth can be opened at 180 degree, a record amongst all vertebrates. The muscles opening the mouth are well developed.

# What is the significance of the large ears of the rabbit?

A rabbit is a small, furry animal with a short tail and pointed ears. It is a weak and timid animal and is always surrounded by many enemies. Therefore, Nature has gifted it with large ears to help it hear, even the slightest sound. The large area of the ear catches almost every sound-wave produced in the air and transfers it into the inner ear. This makes the rabbit aware of its enemies in time and run away to a safe place. A rabbit washes its ears by repeatedly licking its forepaws and rubbing them over the surface of its ears. It does this in order to keep its ears clean. The jackrabbit lives in the desert, where it is very hot in the day and very cold during the night. The long ears of the jackrabbit not only allow it to listen out to enemies, but also help it to control the body temperature. It can lose heat when it is hot or take in heat when it is cold, by controlling the flow of blood through the numerous blood vessels in its large, thin ears.

**BITS OF FACT**

A rabbit has 28 teeth, which keep on growing throughout its life.

# WHAT ARE THE DIFFERENT KINDS OF ANIMALS FOUND IN THE ARCTIC REGION AND HOW HAVE THEY ADAPTED THEMSELVES?



The Arctic is a very cold, windy and often snowy biome located around the North Pole. Animals that live in the Arctic are adapted to extreme conditions. Many animals that live in the Arctic like the Arctic fox and the ermine have coats that thicken and change colour to white during the winter as camouflage in the snow. Some animals hibernate during the cold season; they go into a very deep, sleep-like state in which their heartbeats slow down.

These animals often hibernate in underground burrows or pits. Ground squirrels line their burrows with lichens, leaves and with the hair of musk ox. They, then, roll up these burrows into balls and sleep for seven months. The musk oxen have thick overcoats of shaggy long straight hair that hangs down to the ground. Their undercoats are thick brown fleece. The white fur of the polar bear helps it to sneak up on seals that are laying on the ice packs. Females dig dens in the snow where they hibernate during the worst part of the winter.

### BITS OF FACT

The walrus has to eat thousands of krill and shellfish each day. The layers of blubber protect walruses when they lie out on the ice in the cold wind.

# WHAT IS BAMBOO – TREE OR GRASS?

Bamboo is thought to be a tree but actually it is a kind of grass. It is the largest member of the grass family. Bamboo is the fastest growing woody plant in the world. Its accelerated growth rate (up to 3-4 feet/day) is due to a unique rhizome system and is dependent on local soil and climatic conditions. There are over five hundred types of bamboos. They all consist of smooth, hollow, joined stems with a strong watertight partition at each joint. All grow very quickly. They grow upwards at a rate of 41 centimetres a day and can grow up to a height of 36 metres. While most bamboos flower every year, there are some that flower only three or four times in a century. The flowers are very similar to those of other grasses. The fruits are normally like grasses and some kinds are like nuts. Bamboo has numerous advantages. In the United States, bamboo is mainly used in fishing poles, walking sticks and phonograph needles. Bamboo has long been used to make paper.

### BITS OF FACT

The muli bamboo which grows around the Bay of Bengal flowers every 30-35 years. Its flowering brings disaster as rats multiply to take advantage of the fruits.

# WHAT ARE ALGAE?

Algae are the most primitive form of life. They are simple organisms that live in oceans, lakes, rivers and damp mud. Algae vary in size from single-celled microscopic organisms to huge seaweeds over 60m long. For example, the largest known alga is the giant kelp which grows up to 65m in length. Algae do not have leaves, roots or stems like other plants, but they have chlorophyll in them which enables them to get their energy from sunlight. Algae may be tiny, but they form a vital source of food for sea creatures from shrimps to whales. They also provide most of the oxygen which water creatures need for life. Algae are used by humans in many ways. They are used as fertilizers,

soil conditioners and are a source of livestock feed. Green algae are usually found in freshwater, whereas red or brown algae are found in the warm seas. The chlorophyll of red or brown algae is masked by other pigments.

BITS OF FACT

The blue green algae or the cyanobacteria are the most ancient algae. They appeared on the Earth about 3 million years ago.

# What are the uses of the eucalyptus tree?

Eucalyptus trees make up a group of over 400 species of Australian trees. They grow best in warm places with marked wet and dry seasons. The leaves of the eucalyptus tree are long, narrow and leathery which are cut, pressed and then steamed to make eucalyptus oil. The oil of eucalyptus contains cineole, a potent antiseptic that helps kill bacteria and fungi. It helps increase cardiac action. It is taken in all types of fever. It helps purify blood. It lowers blood sugar. It brings relief to the patients of asthma and bronchitis. The most important tree grown for oil is the blue mallee. The blue gum trees are usually found in North America. Some eucalyptus trees give resins, which are used to protect ships from worms and other animals which make holes in ships. Another Australian eucalyptus tree named jarrah gives red wood which looks like mahogany. Other eucalyptus wood is used to make everything from bats to telegraph poles.

### BITS OF FACT

The tallest tree ever known was the Eucalyptus on River Watts, Victoria, Australia. It measused over 150m in 1872. But the tallest living tree is 112 m high, the Mendocino redwood tree in California.

# WHAT ARE STOMATA?

Stomata are microscopic pores found on the under side of leaves. Stomata are bounded by two half moon-shaped guard cells that function to vary the widths of the pores. Plants carry on the process of photosynthesis by combining together several ingredients in their leaves. Some of these materials are gaseous (carbon dioxide), some are liquid (water) and one is energy (sunlight). The transfer of ingredients occurs, shifting the $CO_2$, light and water from the surrounding atmosphere to the plant. In light, the guard cells swell, causing the pore to be at its widest, and $CO_2$ diffuses into the leaf and into the cells to be assimilated in photosynthesis. In the dark or under drought conditions, the guard cells are not turgid, the stomata are closed and no photosynthesis takes place. Opening of the stomata allows not only $CO_2$ to diffuse into the leaf, but also water vapour to diffuse out of the leaf.

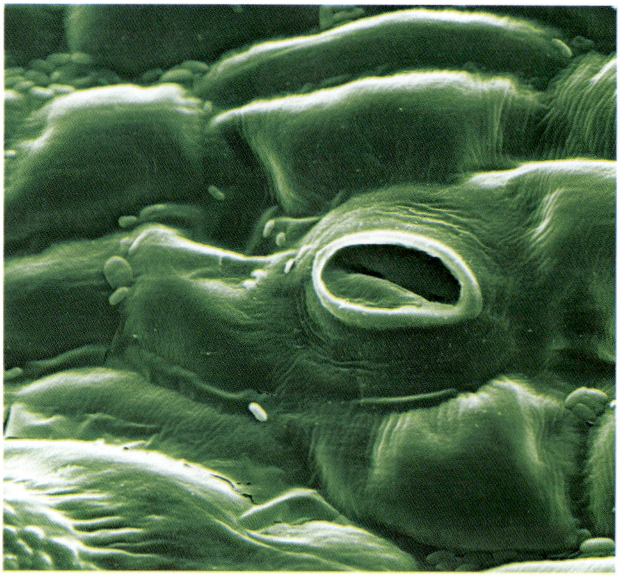

**BITS OF FACT**

In cold autumns, some leaves turn yellow, bright orange or red. This is because the tree responds to cold and reduced sunlight by curtailing chlorophyll production.

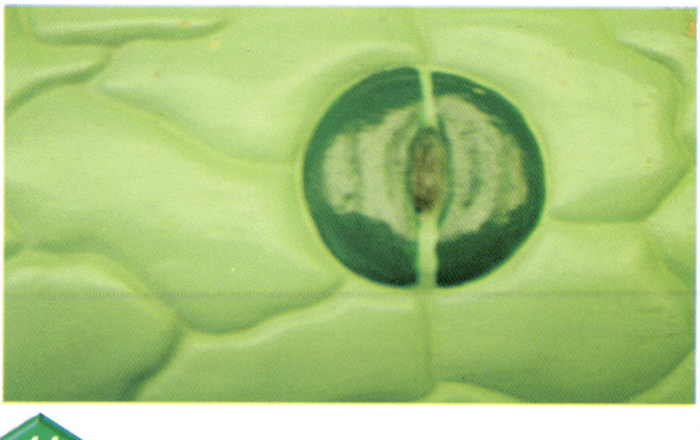

# WHAT IS BONSAI AND HOW SHOULD IT BE TAKEN CARE OF?

Bonsai is literally a plant (usually a tree or shrub) grown in a tray or pot. The first plants grown in pots were in Egypt about 4,000 years ago, mostly for practical reasons, mobility and convenience. The Greeks, the Babylonians, the Persians and the Hindus copied the technique. The Chinese were the first to plant trees in pots for aesthetic purposes about 200 AD. A tree planted in a small pot is not a bonsai until it has been pruned, shaped and trained into the desired shape. Bonsai is kept small by careful control of its growing conditions. Only branches important to the overall design of a bonsai are allowed to remain and unwanted growth is pruned away. Roots are confined to a pot and are periodically clipped. Bonsai usually needs to be watered every day or two. The best time to water is early in the day or late in the afternoon at the same time every day. In general, the soil should be moist, not soaking wet, and not dry. Bonsai must periodically be repotted to supply the pot-bound root system with fresh soil.

**BITS OF FACT**

The word bonsai is derived from two Chinese characters, meaning a tree planted in a shallow container. The word is pronounced "bone-sigh"

# WHAT IS GRAFTING?

Grafting is a method of plant propagation widely used in horticulture (gardening), where the tissues of one plant are encouraged to fuse with those of another. It is most commonly used for the propagation of trees and shrubs grown commercially. A part of one plant is connected to a part of another plant; the two, then, grow together to become a single plant. The top part, which will produce the branches, leaves, flowers, and fruit, is known as the "scion". The lower portion, which produces the root system and the very bottom part of the trunk, is known as the rootstock. The scar where the two are joined, and which may remain visible throughout the life of the tree, is the graft union. For successful grafting to take place, the vascular cambium tissues of the stock and scion plants must be placed in contact with each other. Both tissues must be kept alive until the graft has taken, usually a period of a few weeks.

## BITS OF FACT

Tree branches and more often roots of the some species will sometimes naturally graft, this is called inosculation. When roots make physical contact with each other, they often grow together.

# What are Herbs?

Herbs are fragrant leaves and stems of plants whose stems are not woody (exceptions like rosemary). They are small plants whose leaves can be used to make medicines, food or perfumes. Most herbs are perennial and have soft stems. Basil, a sweet mild herb which has a peppery taste, is used in salads. Sage is another which is thought to have special healing qualities. Its leaves are used fresh or dried. It is also a great flavouring for meat. Rosemary is a coastal plant and is believed to improve memory. Thyme is another herb which comes from the Mediterranean. It is very strong and spicy and is mainly used fresh or dried. It is one of the best herbs for seafood, but can be used with poultry, meat and vegetables too. Parsley thyme and a bay leaf may be tied in a muslin cloth and hung in soups while cooking to give them extra flavours.

## BITS OF FACT

Bay leaves are the leaves of an evergreen laurel tree. They were used to make crowns for athletes, heroes and poets in Ancient Rome. It is also said that a bay tree planted by a person in the verandah of his/her home protects the home from lightning.

# WHAT ARE THE DIFFERENT KINDS OF NUTS?



A nut is a fruit with a single seed in which the outside has gone hard. Actually it is a seed wrapped in a hard shell. Nuts are a concentrated, nutritious food which contains 10-20% protein and 50% fat. Peanuts contain more food energy than sugar and more proteins, minerals and

vitamins. Almonds come from trees native to South West Asia, but are now grown all over the world. The almond tree with white flowers produces bitter almonds, which are used in the manufacture of drugs used in medicines. Sweet almonds come from the tree with pink blossoms, which are grown in abundance in western Asia, Mediterranean regions and in California. Coconut was previously grown along the East Indies Coast and in the South Sea. But now, it is found in the tropics of all continents. Coconut is rich in protein. Its oil is used in cooking. The brazil nut is very hard to crack, but very delicious. It grows in clusters of twenty or more tightly packed in a hard, round shell.

**BITS OF FACT**

Pistachios aren't actually nuts. It's true. Pistachio "nuts" are actually seeds of red or yellow plum-like fruits whose flesh is removed during processing.

# What causes the difference between the tastes of fruits?

Each fruit has a different taste which varies in some way from the taste of any other fruit. The taste of any fruit depends on the compounds it bears. In general, a fruit consists of fructose (natural sugar), organic acids, vitamins, starch, proteins, minerals and cellulose. All these materials are present in different proportions in different fruits. Fruits having more fructose-content taste sweeter, while those having more acids taste sour. Orange is a fruit which comprises almost equal quantities of fructose and acids. Hence, it tastes both sweet and sour. In general, raw fruits contain more acids, but on ripening, the quantity of acid decreases and the amount of sugar increases. Therefore, raw mangoes are sour, but ripe ones are sweet. Some fruits, like lemons, do not taste sweet even after ripening. This is because of the excessive amount of acids.

**BITS OF FACT**

About 32 million tonnes of apples are packed every year around the world. Half are eaten fresh and a quarter are made into the alcoholic drink cider. The USA is the world's leading producer of cider apples.

# WHAT ARE FUNGI?

Fungi are not plants, because they have no chlorophyll to make their food. They are a group of 50,000 species which include mushrooms, toadstools, mould, mildew and yeast. Since fungi cannot make their own food, they live on other plants and animals as parasites. Fungi are made of numerous thread-like structures called hyphae, which absorb the chemicals they feed on. Fungi feed on the host by releasing chemicals called enzymes, which break down chemicals in their host. Fungi which live on living organisms are called parasitic fungi, whereas fungi which live on dead plants and animals are called saprophytic. The most poisonous of all fungi is the destroying angel. It can kill anyone who eats it once. Fly agaric is a toadstool which is a poisonous mushroom. It is easy to recognize from its spotted red cap. The field mushroom grown wild or cultivated is the mushroom most widely eaten.

**BITS OF FACT**

Penicillin is a life-saving antibiotic drug which is made from mould fungi.

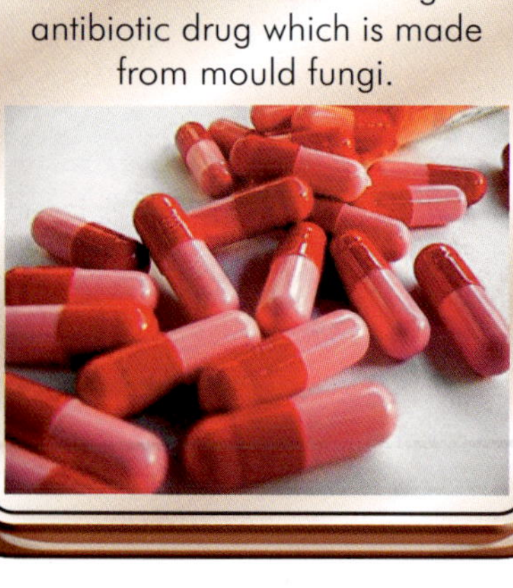

# WHAT IS THE IMPORTANCE OF PLANTS?

Plants are helpful for the survival of human beings in several ways. They not only provide us with food, but also give us oxygen to survive. Plants consume carbon dioxide which we release and give off oxygen which human beings require to survive. Shampoos, perfumes, bath oils and creams are made from sweet-smelling plants. The corks that seal the bottles of wine are made from the bark (cork) of the oak tree. Besides this, plants help us to make lots of useful things such as paper, cloth and medicines. The coal which we use today comes from plants which grew even before dinosaurs existed. Trees also provide us with fuel, timber, resins, varnishes, dyes, rubber and many more things. Softwood is obtained from coniferous trees such as pine, larch, fir and spruce. 75-80% of the natural forests of northern Asia, Europe and the USA are softwood. Hardwood timber is obtained from broad-leaved trees like the oak.

**BITS OF FACT**

About three billion cubic metres of wood is used every year throughout the world. This means that if a pile was made, it would cover a football stadium as high as Mt Everest.

# WHAT IS BARK AND WHAT ARE ITS USES?

The outer covering of the stem of woody plants is known as bark. It is composed of waterproof cork cells. One of its main function is to shield the inner and more soft structures of the tree. It not only keeps them from drying out but also protects them against outside injuries. The bark protects a layer of food-conducting tissue called the phloem or inner bark. The process by which bark is formed may continue year after year. As the woody stem increases in size, the outer bark of the dead cork cells give way; it may split to form grooves or shed off or peel off. A layer of reproductive cells, called the cork cambium, produces new cork cells to replace the old ones. The bark of the hemlock tree is used in the tanning of leather. Bottle corks are made from the thick, spongy bark of the cork oak, which grows in the Mediterranean region. Quinine is made from the bark of the cinchona tree. Extracts from the bark of other trees are used for flavouring and as medicines.

**BITS OF FACT**

The spice cinnamon is the powdered bark of a tree which is grown in India and Malaya.

# WHAT ARE LICHENS?

Lichens are a wonderful partnership of algae and fungi. There are about 20,000 species of lichens. They are usually flat and crust-like, with no roots or stems. They often grow on roofs or soil, but most grow on rocks or the branches of trees. The algae in lichens make food from sunlight to feed the fungi, whereas the fungi make a protective layer around the algae and hold water. Lichens can grow only when moistened by rain. They grow very slowly, but can eventually cover very large areas. Some lichens grow a fraction of a millimeters in a year. Lichens could survive in many places where other plants would die, for example, the Arctic, deserts and mountain tops. Some Arctic lichens are believed to be 4,000 years old. Lichens are very sensitive to air pollution, especially sulphur dioxide. Hence, they are used by scientists to indicate air pollution. Scandinavian reindeer moss is a lichen eaten by reindeers. It is also exported to Germany for decorations.

**BITS OF FACT**

The oakmoss lichen from Europe and North Africa is added to most perfumes and after shaves to stop the flower scents from fading.

# WHAT ARE THE DIFFERENT PARTS OF A FLOWER?

Flowers are the reproductive organs of a plant. Usually, flowers have both the male and female reproductive parts. The male reproductive part consists of stamens, which are made up of filaments and anthers. Filaments are tiny stalks which hold anthers. These anthers produce tiny dust-like grains called pollen. The female reproductive part consists of the carpel which is made up of style, stigma, ovary and ovules. The ovary is hidden in a bulb-shaped receptacle at the base of the flower. Inside the ovary are one or more ovules, which become seeds if the flower is not fertilized. In order for a flower to be fertilized, pollen must be transferred from the male stamen to the female stigma. That is why flowers are colourful and scented so that bees may be attracted towards them to carry

## BITS OF FACT

The world's largest flower is the Rafflesia, which is found in the jungles of south-east Asia. This flower with orange-brown and white petals often reaches a diameter of about 90 cm with a thickness of about 2 cm.

# WHAT ARE THE USES OF THE WILLOW TREE?

Willow trees are usually found in moist habitats such as flood plains and on river banks. These trees grow very rapidly in this climate. The willow tree is very useful in several ways. Its leaves provide food for the wildlife. The leaves and bark of the willow tree have been mentioned in ancient texts from Assyria, Sumer and Egypt as a remedy for aches and fever. The bark of the willow tree contains an active compound salicin, which is used in making many medicines. Aspirin is a derivative of salicylic acid, which was synthesized from derivatives of the willow bark. The twigs of the common osier are grown for the use in basket making, whereas the light but dent-resistant wood of other willow trees is used in making artificial limbs, wooden shoes and cricket bats, brooms, cradles, boards, chairs and other furniture, dolls, flutes, poles, toys, tool handles, wands and whistles.

## BITS OF FACT

Some willows (particularly arctic and alpine species), are low-growing or creeping shrubs, for example: the dwarf willow rarely exceeds 6 cm in height. Yet, it spreads widely across the ground.

# What do you mean by seaweeds?

The term seaweed refers to the large marine algae that grow almost exclusively in the shallow waters at the edge of the world's oceans. They provide home and food for many different sea animals, lend beauty to the underwater landscape and are directly valuable to man as food and industrial raw material. Seaweeds can make their own food with the help of sunlight, but they are devoid of roots, stems, leaves and flowers. Instead of roots, seaweeds have 'holdfasts' which look like roots, Seaweeds may be red, green or brown algae. Red algae are small and fern- like and grow 30-60 metres down in the tropical seas. Brown algae like the giant kelp are big, but grow down to about 20 metres only, usually in cold waters. Gulfweed floats so densely on the Sargasso Sea which covers an area of 5.2 million square km east of West Indies that it looks like a green meadow.

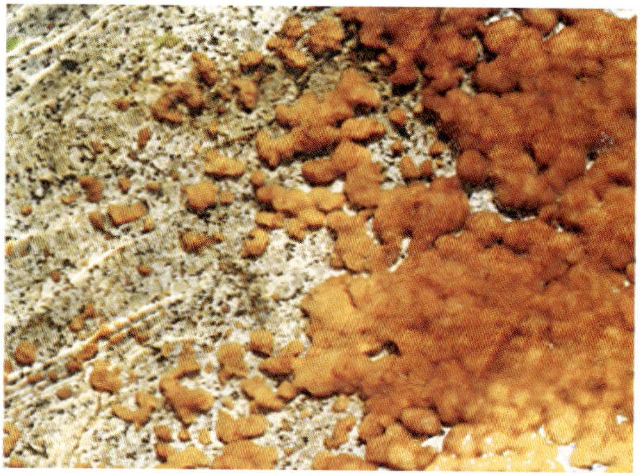

## BITS OF FACT

The giant kelp is the fastest growing plant in the sea. It can grow about 1 metre in a single day and can grow up to 60 metres long.

# WHAT ARE THE DIFFERENT KINDS OF ROSES?

Roses are one of the most popular garden flowers. This is because of their lovely perfumes and beautiful blooms. Wild roses have smaller flowers with usually single layers of five petals. Garden roses have big flowers with sets of five petals in two or more layers. There are about 100 species of wild roses, but all the present-day garden roses were created by crossing 10 Asian species. Today, there are about 13,000 varieties of garden roses. Garden roses are divided on the basis of their time to bloom. Old roses bloom only once in a year in early summer, for example: yellow briers, damask roses etc. Perpetual roses bloom twice in early summer and in autumn, for example: hybrid perpetuals. Ever-blooming hybrids bloom all summer , such as floribundas, hybrid teas, gloribundas and polyanthas. Attar of roses is a perfume made from roses, especially damask roses.

## BITS OF FACT

One of the most popular rose is the Peace of the Hybrid Teas. These hybrid teas were created by crossing the ever blooming, fragile tea roses with the vigorous perpetuals.

# WHAT DO YOU MEAN BY CARNIVOROUS PLANTS?



Carnivorous plants are those plants which trap insects for their food. These plants survive in places where the availability of nitrogen is insufficient. Hence, they eat insects to fulfil the quantity of nitrogen required. An insect is lured into the jaw-like leaf trap of the Venus fly trap with nectar. Once the insect has landed, the jaws shut on the victim in a fraction of a second. Immediately, the plant secretes juices that drown and then dissolve the insect. The leaves of the sundew are covered in tentacles that ooze a sticky substance known as mucilage. Insects are trapped in its tentacles and are then suffocated within ten seconds. The pitcher plant is another carnivorous plant. The inside of the tubular shaped leaf is lined with downward pointing hair. The hair blocks an insect from climbing up the tube and escaping. The fluid in the bottom of the tube contains digestive juices that digest the prey.

### BITS OF FACT

The bladders of the bladderwort were once thought to be air sacs to keep the plant afloat. In fact, they are tiny traps for water insects.

# What is the Earth's atmosphere made up of?

The atmosphere is a blanket of gases which extends around the Earth. The atmosphere is made up of 78% nitrogen, 21% oxygen, 1% argon and carbon dioxide and tiny traces of neon, krypton, zenon, helium, methane and carbon monoxide. The atmosphere is divided into five layers – exosphere, thermosphere, mesosphere, stratosphere and troposphere. The exosphere is the highest level of the atmosphere, which means that gas is very sparse. In the thermosphere, temperatures are very high, ranging from -120 degrees Centigrade to 2,000 degrees Centigrade about 700 km up. The mesosphere contains few gases, but it is thick enough to slow down meteorites. Temperatures range between 10 degrees Centigrade to -120 degrees Centigrade about 80 km up. The stratosphere is completely calm and clear. That is why jet airliners fly in this layer. Temperatures range from -60 degrees Centigrade to 10 degrees Centigrade about 50 km up. Although the troposhere is just 12 km thick yet it contains 75 % of the weight of gases in the atmosphere. Temperature drops by height from 18 degrees Centigrade to -60 degrees Centigrade .

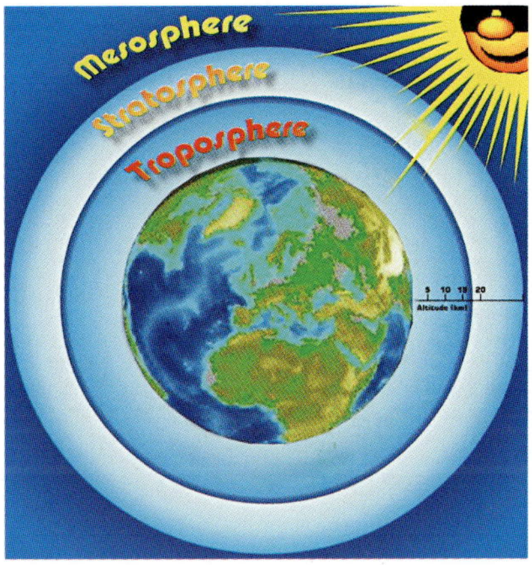


**BITS OF FACT**

The troposhere is the layer in which we live. The stratosphere contains the ozone layer, which protects us from the Sun's ultraviolet rays. Low level satellites orbit in the exosphere.

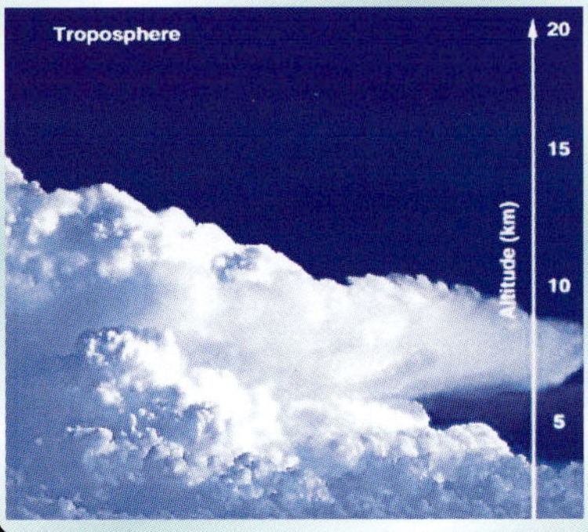

AMAZING EARTH

# WHAT ARE DAMS?

Dams are very strong, thick walls built across rivers to hold back the water. Dams are manly built for water supply, irrigation, electric power, flood control and also for the improvement of navigation. Dams that deal with irrigation store the water and supply the crops with it when the going gets tough. Some dams can direct the water into pipelines and other irrigation instruments. There are also water supply dams. These dams supply the large cities with water. Flood control dams keep the river from overflowing. They release the water at the bottom of the dams. In this way, they can control the water below. There are also navigation dams. These are built so that a ship may have the right depth of water. The passage of a river may be blocked by a waterfall or rapids. Some dams are built to generate power. Hydroelectric dams do just the same job. They direct the water into turbines.

**BITS OF FACT**

Tehri Dam on River Bhagirathi is the highest dam in India. With a height of 261 metres, Tehri Dam is the sixth highest dam in the world.

# WHAT IS SAND AND WHAT ARE ITS USES?

Sand is a rock material that has been eroded by river action into tiny grains. Theoretically, sand could be composed of any eroded rock, but it is largely made up of quartz because quartz is a very hard substance and so does not erode easily. Sand is made of minerals and tiny pieces of rock that have come from the erosion and weathering of rocks. The composition of sand varies from place to place depending on the sources and conditions of the local rocks. One specific form of sand is the major ingredient in glass-making. Other types of sand are used in foundries to make casting moulds and in ceramics, plasters and cement. Sand is also used as a grinding and polishing abrasive in the form of sandwater. Brick manufactu-ring plants use sand as an additive with a mixture of clay and other materials for manufacturing bricks. Sand is sometimes mixed with paint to create a textured finish for walls and ceilings or a non-slip floor surface.

**BITS OF FACT**

The Sahara is probably the world's most famous desert. Sandstorms are common in the Sahara and the walls of sand can reach up to 6,000 metres high.

# WHAT IS SO SPECIAL ABOUT RIVER HWANG HO ?

River Hwang Ho in China is the muddiest river in the world. It is also known as Yellow River. It is the second-longest river in China after River Yangtze and the sixth-longest in the world at 5,464 kilometres. It originates in the Bayankala Mountains in Qinghai Province in western China. It flows through the nine provinces of China and empties into the Bohai Sea. The river gets its yellow colour mostly from the fine-grained calcareous silts which originate in the Loess Plateau and are carried in the flow. It carries so much silt that you could build a vast wall 40m high and 6 m wide all round the world. Silt deposition and dyking over the centuries has caused the river to flow above the surrounding farmland, making flooding a critically dangerous problem. Yellow River carries 1.6 billion tons of silt into the sea annually.

## BITS OF FACT

It is believed that the Chinese civilization originated in Yellow riven basin. The Chinese refer to the river as 'the mother river' and 'the cradle of the Chinese' civilization.

# WHAT IS ACID RAIN?



Acid rain refers to any form of precipitation with high levels of nitric and sulphuric acids. It can also occur in the form of snow, fog and tiny bits of dry material that settle to the Earth. Rotting vegetation and erupting volcanoes release some chemicals that can cause acid rain, but most acid rain falls because of human activities. The biggest culprit is the burning of fossil fuels by coal-burning power plants, factories and automobiles. When humans burn fossil fuels, sulphur dioxide and nitrogen oxides are released into the atmosphere. These chemical gases react with water, oxygen and other substances to form the mild solutions of sulphuric and nitric acids. When acid rain reaches the Earth, it flows across the surface and sinks into the soil. Acid rain has many ecological effects; it makes water acidic and causes it to absorb the aluminium that makes its way from soil into lakes and streams. This combination makes waters toxic to crayfish, clams, fish and other aquatic animals. Acid rain also damages forests, especially those at higher elevations. It robs the soil of essential nutrients and releases aluminium in the soil, which makes it hard for trees to take up water.

## BITS OF FACT

Coal, oil and natural gas are called fossil fuels. Crude oil reserves are found all over the world, but the Middle East alone has about 63 per cent of the known reserves.

# WHAT MAKES THE GREAT SPHINX OF GIZA SO SIGNIFICANT?

The Great Sphinx of Giza is so significant because it is the largest structure created from a single piece of stone. It is 20m high, 57m long and 6m wide. The Great Sphinx of Giza is a half-human, half-lion Sphinx statue in Egypt on the Giza Plateau at the west bank of River Nile, near modern-day Cairo. The commonly-held belief is that it was created during the 2700s BC. According to others, it is believed to have been created at the will of King Khafra, whose pyramid the sphinx happens to be situated in front. The material of the Sphinx is the limestone bedrock which originated fifty million years ago from sediments deposited at the bottom of sea waters that engulfed northeast Africa during the Middle Eocene period. All of the significant major pyramids were built over a time period of about 200 years. There were three tunnels built in the Sphinx, but the passage of time has left the destinations unreachable and the tunnels themselves seem to stop short.

## BITS OF FACT

The Great Pyramid of Khufu is by far the most famous Pyramid in Egypt. It is the biggest, tallest and the most intact. After its construction, it became one of the "Seven Wonders Of The World". Today, it is the only one of them which still survives.

# WHAT DOES THE OCEAN LOOK LIKE?

The ocean is made up of 60 different chemical elements that give it its salty taste. The main ingredients, chlorine, sodium, sulphate, magnesium, calcium and potassium, come mostly from river sediments & dumped into the ocean. The temperature of the water differs according to the intensity of the Sun's rays hitting it. The surface of water is warmer than that at a great depth. The colours that make up sunlight are absorbed in different ways by water particles. Red, yellow and orange cannot penetrate more than a few feet below the surface of water. Blue can penetrate more than 800 feet. That is why the ocean appears blue. Sometimes water looks green. It is because it contains several tiny plants called phytoplankton. Water puts pressure on the human body. The deeper we go, the greater the pressure. The Black Sea and the Yellow Sea get their names from the colour of sediment floating in their water and lying on their beds.

**BITS OF FACT**

The Red Sea gets its name from the red algae that occasionally appear on its surface.

# WHAT ARE THE DIFFERENT TYPES OF VOLCANOES?



A volcano is an opening or rupture in a planet's surface or crust, which allows hot, molten rock, ash and gases to escape from below the surface. The different types of volcanoes are:-

Composite volcanoes, also called strato volcanoes, are formed by alternating layers of lava and rock fragments. Strato volcanoes are usually large and conical.

Shield volcanoes may be produced by hot spots which lay far away from the edges of tectonic plates. The eruptions of shield volcanoes are characterized by low-explosivity lava-fountaining that forms cinder cones and spatter cones at the vent.

**BITS OF FACT**

The largest volcano is Mauna Loa, in Hawaii. The tallest is Mauna Kea which, when measured from its base on the ocean floor, is more than 30,000 feet high.

Cinder cones are not famous as their eruptions usually don't cause any loss of life. They rarely exceed 250m in height and 500m in diameter.

When hot erupting lava contains just enough explosive gas to prevent the formation of a lava – flow, but not enough to shatter it into small fragments, the lava is torn by expanding gases into fluid hot clots, ranging in size from 1cm to 50cm across. Such volcanoes are called spatter volcanoes.

A volcano that consists of a complex of two or more vents is known as a compound or complex volcano.

# What is a hill?

A simple definition of a hill is a high ground up to 307 m high. Above this height, it is a mountain. Mountains are solid rocks whereas hills can be solid rocks or piles of debris built up by glaciers or wind. Hills that are solid rocks are very old, having been worn down from mountains over millions of years. Hills may be created by faults. Faults are a slight crack in the earth which can cause earthquakes. Hills are formed when these faults go slightly upwards. Hills are also formed by the deep erosion of areas that were raised by disturbances in the earth's crust. Erosion forms hills by carrying away all of the soil on a mountain, causing a hill to be left behind. Volcanoes form hills when they erupt. During the eruption, volcanic ash is spewed through the air. After the eruption, the lava or molten rock hardens and builds up a thick layer of lava rock. The ash falls on the hardened lava causing a layer of ash to form on the hill. When rain falls, this layer of ash mixes with the rainwater to form black coloured water. This black water freezes causing the lava rock to crack and crumble and eventually erodes to form a hill.

**BITS OF FACT**

The Black Hills of South Dakota hold two national caves: Wind Cave National Park and Jewel Cave National Monument. Jewel Cave is presently the fourth largest cave in the world.

# What are tectonic plates?

The Earth's surface is divided into thick slabs called tectonic plates. Each plate is a fragment of the Earth's rigid outer layer or lithosphere. There are 16 large plates and several smaller ones. The plates are made of rock and are from 50 to 150 km thick. They move both horizontally and vertically. The Pacific plate is the biggest plate which covers the whole of the Pacific Ocean. It is continuously in motion; it moves by about 10 cm a year. It takes hundreds of millions of years for it to move vast distances. The Pacific plate is the only large plate which has no continent situated on it. The movement of the tectonic plates is responsible for several things, which include the pattern of volcanic and earthquake activity around the world. Most of the Earth's seismic activity (volcanos and earthquakes) occurs at the plate boundaries as they interact. The top layers of the plates are called the crust. Oceanic crust (the crust under the oceans) is thinner and denser than continental crust.

**BITS OF FACT**

Plate Tectonics is a theory which was originally invented by the German geologist Alfred Wegener in the 1930s.

# WHAT ARE WETLANDS?

Wetlands are areas of land where the water level is mostly above the ground. Bogs, fens, swamps and marshes are the main types of wetland. Wetlands act like sponges and help to control floods as well as to top up supplies of groundwater. Bogs and fens occur in cold climates and contain plenty of partially rotted plant material called peat. Marshes and swamps are found in cold and warm places. They have more plants than bogs and fens. A swamp is a cross between a lake and land. Although its waters are usually very shallow yet lots of special kinds of trees and plants can be found growing in the water. A marsh is drier than a swamp and water cannot always be seen, but the ground and the plants that grow in it are always soggy or waterlogged. Reeds and rushes grow in marshes. Wetlands provide a safe and lush environment for many different species of fish, birds and insects. There are many types of vegetation in wetlands. There are plants such as cattails, bulrushes, sedges, arrowhead, water lilies, blue flag and floaters like common duckweed.

**BITS OF FACT**

Trees such as mangroves grow in swamps. They further stabilize sediment and over time increase the soil level. This results in less tidal movement and the development of salt marshes.

## What is the speciality of Uluru?

Uluru, formerly known as Ayers Rock, is the world's largest monolith or single piece of stone on the planet. It rises from the broad desert plain in the deep centre of Australia. Uluru/Ayers Rock is Australia's most recognizable natural icon. The famous sandstone monolith stands 348 metres high and has an elliptical shape with a circumference of 9.4 kilometres. Like an iceberg, it has most of its bulk below the surface. It is located 440 kilometres south-west of Alice Springs in the Uluru-Kata Tjuta National Park. Uluru is particularly notable for its striking appearance at different times of the year as it appears to change colours with the different light angles at different times of the day and year. Sunset is a particularly remarkable sight when it briefly glows red.

Although rainfall is uncommon in this semiarid area yet, during wet periods, the rock acquires a silvery-grey colour, with streaks of black algae forming on the areas that serve as channels for water flow. This massive pile of rock dome dates back to 500 million years.

**BITS OF FACT**

The Sydney Opera House in Australia is a great architectural work of the 20th century. It represents multiple strands of creativity, both in architectural form and structural design.

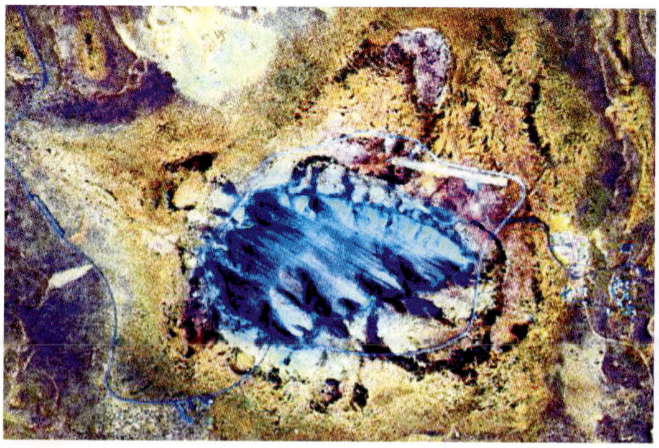

# WHAT ARE THE DIFFERENT ZONES OF THE OCEAN?

The uppermost layer of the world's oceans is called the sunlit zone or the euphotic zone. The depth of this zone depends on the clarity of the water. In clear water, the euphotic zone can be quite deep. In murky water, it can be only 50 feet deep. On average, it extends to about 200 metres, the depth of the ocean averages about 4,000 m. The temperature in this zone ranges from 104 to 27 degrees F. In this zone, there is enough light for photosynthesis to take place. Many plants and other photo-synthetic organisms live in this zone and food is abundant. The middle layer of the world's oceans receives only faint, filtered sunlight during the daytime. This barely-lit ocean layer is called the twilight zone or the disphotic zone. This zone appears deep blue to black in colour. The disphotic zone extends to about 1,000 m deep. On an average, this zone extends from 200 to 1,000 m. There is not enough light for photosynthesis to take place. So, no plants live in this zone. The third zone or the aphotic zone lies beyond 1,000 m. In this region, less than 1% of sunlight penetrates and the temperatures range from 0 - 6°C (32 - 43°F).

## BITS OF FACT

Unusual and unique creatures dwell in the expanse of pitch black water or the aphotic zone, such as the gulper eel, the giant squid, the anglerfish and the vampire squid.

# What are the animals found in the aphotic zone?

The aphotic zone begins at a depth of 3,000 ft and continues to the bottom, which usually maxes out at a depth of 18,000 ft. In the aphotic zone, photosynthesis cannot occur. So, plants and cyanobacteria are absent. Instead, animals have to subsist on carcasses that fall from above. Some animals that live in the aphotic zone include the gulper eel, the giant squid, smaller squids, anglerfish, vampire squid and numerous jellyfish. Some of the ugliest and most evil-looking fish in the world are found here, including the viper fish, the fangtooth, the dragonfish, the lizardfish and many others. These fish often have hinged jaws, black scales, piercing eyes and extremely sharp teeth. Many of the animals in the aphotic zone are bioluminescent, meaning they can produce their own light in one way or another. This can be used both for navigation and luring small animals into their jaws. The anglerfish is probably the most famous example as it has a lure protruding in front of its mouth from a special appendage on its head. Other bottom-feeders include the aptly-named blobfish, coffin fish (which walk along the sea floor using leg-like fins) and the others. At the bottom, one can also find sea cucumbers and giant isopods.

**BITS OF FACT**

The deep sea also has numerous unusual and rare sharks, such as the Megamouth Shark, hailed as one of the most impressive marine animal discoveries of the last century.

# What are the different types of coral reefs?

Coral reefs are massive structures formed from coral polyps, tiny animals that live in colonies. The different types of reefs include: Fringing reefs occur along a rocky coastline where corals remain extended outwards from the shore. They form an outermost line or ridge that runs parallel to the shore.

In certain conditions, coral reefs develop far from the continents, around small islands, or towards the edge of the continental shelf. Here, the reefs do not join up to the mainland, but grow upwards on all sides. These large, elongated structures far offshore are called barrier reefs. Coral atolls begin as fringing reefs around active oceanic volcanoes. When the volcanic eruptions cease, an island remains. Over long geological periods, the island begins to sink. The fringing reef continues to grow as the island sinks. Soon, the fringing reef around the shore becomes a barrier reef separated from the shrinking island by a deeper lagoon. After thousands of years, the volcanic island sinks completely below the sea level, but the corals continue to grow, forming a circular coral reef, an atoll.

## BITS OF FACT

When you go to Australia, you just cannot miss seeing the Great Barrier Reef. It is the world's largest coral reef and extends for over 1,200 km. It lies a short distance from the north-east coast.

# WHAT IS SO SACRED ABOUT THE SHWEDAGON PAGODA ?

Shwedagon Pagoda is the most popular and well-known pagoda in Yangon, Myanmar (Burma). The legend of the Shwedagon the Pagoda begins with two Burmese merchant brothers who met the Buddha. The Buddha gave them eight of his hairs to be enshrined in Burma. The great Shwedagon Pagoda stands on a platform covering over 5 hectares on a hill 58m above the sea level. The platform is full of glittering, colourful stupas, but the huge main stupa is the centre of attention for most pilgrims. The stupa is completely solid, every inch is covered in gold, and the upper parts are studded with diamonds totalling over 2,000 carats. The main stupa is supported on a square plinth that stands 6.4m above the platform, setting it apart from the other stupas. On this raised platform are smaller stupas: large ones on the four cardinal directions, medium ones at the four corners and 60 small ones around the perimeter. Topping the stupa is the spectacular hti (spire decoration), which has seven tiers. Made of iron and covered in gold plates, the hti weighs well over a ton. Gold bells, silver bells and various jewellery are added to this.

**BITS OF FACT**

At the very top of the spire is the diamond orb – a hollow gold sphere studded with 4,351 diamonds totalling 1,800 carats. On the very tip rests a single, 76-carat diamond.

# What is an Aquifer?

When rain falls, some of the water goes straight into rivers and lakes, but most of the water is soaked by the soil and reaches the rocks below. If the rock does not allow the rain water to pass through, an underground river is formed. Where the rain water flows through rocks, pockets of water, called aquifers, develop. In other words, an aquifer is a layer of rock or sediment through which water moves easily. Sandstone, chalk and limestone are good aquifers because these rocks have tiny gaps or pores through which water flows. Some aquifers have been filling up for thousands of years and are like huge underground reservoirs. Wells are drilled into these rocks and water is pumped out. Sometimes the porous rock layers become tilted in the earth. There might be a confining layer of less porous rock both above and below the porous layer. This is an example of a confined aquifer. An oasis is a moist, fertile area of a desert where an aquifer is close to the surface.

**BITS OF FACT**

Metamorphic rocks are created when other types of rocks are transformed due to great pressure and heat within the earth. For example, marble is formed when limestone comes under great pressure.

# What is Mount Erebus?

Mt Erebus, situated in Ross Island, Antarctica, is the world's southernmost active volcano. Discovered in 1841 by James Ross, it is one of only a very few volcanoes in the world with a long-lived lava lake. Ross Island is entirely volcanic in origin and is formed by four principal volcanoes – Mount Erebus, Terror, Bird and Terra Nova- as well as numerous smaller volcanoes and lava flows. Of the volcanoes, only Erebus remains active. At 3,794 metres, Mount Erebus is the highest point on Ross Island and the largest, most active volcano on Antarctica continent. It is almost always observed with a cloud of vapour rising from its summit crater. Much eruptive and seismic activity has been observed, including the ejections of volcanic bombs as much as 8 metres across. At the summit, a 100-metre-deep outer crater about 650 metres across, contains a similarly deep inner crater about 250 metres across, in which lies a lake of red, molten lava.

**BITS OF FACT**

It has been estimated that during the feeding season in Antarctica, a full grown blue whale eats about 4 million krill per day (krill are small shrimp-like creatures).

# WHAT IS A FAX MACHINE?

A fax machine is a device that can send or receive pictures and text over a telephone line. Fax machines have been around in one form or another for more than a century but it was Alexander Bain who patented the first fax design in 1843. A fax machine consists of an optical scanner for digitizing images on paper, a printer for printing incoming fax messages and a telephone for making the connection. Fax machines work by digitizing an image – dividing it into a grid of dots. Each dot is either on or off, depending on whether it is black or white. Electronically, each dot is represented by a bit that has a value of either 0 (off) or 1 (on). In this way, the fax machine translates a picture into a series of zeros and ones (called a bit map) that can be transmitted like normal computer data. On the receiving side, a fax machine reads the incoming data, translates the zeros and ones back into dots and reprints the picture. While sending documents to people at large distances, faxes have a distinct advantage over postal mail in respect that the delivery is instantaneous.

**BITS OF FACT**

Nokia Corporation is currently the world`s largest manufacturer of cell phones.

# WHAT IS A BUNSEN BURNER?

A Bunsen burner is a laboratory device designed to heat substances for various experiments. It is a gas burner used in laboratories because it provides a hot, steady, smokeless flame. Bunsen burner was invented

by Robert Wilhelm Bunsen in 1855. Bunsen (31st March, 1811-16th August, 1899) was a German chemist and teacher. He invented the Bunsen burner for his research in isolating chemical substances. Peter Desaga who passed from the University of Heidelberg (where Bunsen worked) was a mechanic. He built the first Bunsen burner to Bunsen's specifications. The design of a Bunsen burner includes a vertical metal tube which is connected to a weighted base. The base includes a nozzle to connect with a fuel source, as well as a gas valve and a flame adjuster to control how much air is admitted through small air-holes at the base of the tube. The gas mixes with air at the bottom of the tube and then rises to the top of the Bunsen burner, where it can be lit with a matchstick or lighter.

## BITS OF FACT

The modern match was invented by a British chemist John Walker in 1827. The cigarette lighter was invented 11 years prior in 1816 by a German chemist named J.W. Dobereine.

# WHAT IS RADAR?

Radar (Radio Detection And Ranging) is a system that uses electromagnetic waves to identify the range, altitude, direction or speed of both moving and fixed objects such as aircraft, ships, motor vehicles. Radar signals bounce off objects in their path and the radar system detects the echoes of signals that return. Radar can determine a number of properties of a distant object, such as its distance, speed, direction of motion and shape. One of the primary uses of radar is air traffic control, both civilian and military. Large networks of ground-based radar systems help air traffic controllers keep track of aircraft and prevent midair collisions. Military forces around the world use radar to detect aircraft and missiles, troop movement and ships at sea, as well as to target various types of weapons. Meteorologists use radar to observe and forecast the weather. Other scientists use radar for mapping the surface of the earth from orbit, studying asteroids, and investigating the surfaces of other planets and their moons.

**BITS OF FACT**

The parabolic antenna is a high-gain reflector antenna used for radio, television and data communications, and also for radiolocation.

# WHAT IS THE INTERNET?

The Internet, sometimes called simply "the Net," is a worldwide system of computer networks in which users at any computer can, if they have permission, get information from any other computer and can also talk directly to users at other computers. The Internet is composed of many interconnected computer networks. Each network may link tens, hundreds, or even thousands of computers, enabling them to share information and processing power.

The Internet has made it possible for people all over the world to communicate with one another effectively and inexpensively. Unlike traditional broadcasting media, such as radio and television, the Internet does not have a centralized distribution system. Instead, an individual who has Internet access can communicate directly with anyone else on the Internet, post information for general consumption, retrieve information, use distant applications and services, or buy and sell products. Each computer connected up to the Internet has software called TCP/IP (Transmission Control rotocol/Internet Protocol) which is responsible for receiving, sending and checking information.

## BITS OF FACT

A webcam or web camera is a term used for any camera that generates images which can be accessed by and displayed on the world wide web through a server.

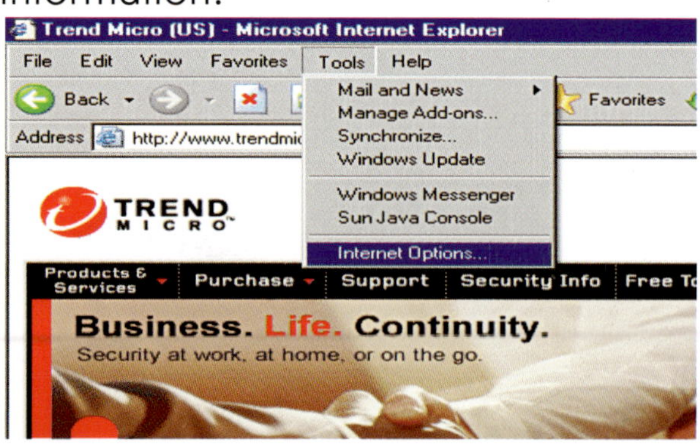

# WHAT ARE LASERS?

The word LASER is an acronym for Light Amplification by Stimulated Emission of Radiation which describes the process by which lasers generate visible, ultraviolet or infrared emissions. A laser is a device that creates and amplifies a narrow, intense beam of coherent light. The light produced by a laser has very different properties to that produced by other sources (such as the sun, light bulbs and fluorescent or neon tubes). Laser light is monochromatic (a single wavelength) and typically confined to a narrow beam which spreads slightly with distance. Thus, the energy carried by a laser beam is concentrated in a small area and can travel efficiently over large distances. Lasers are widely used in industry for cutting and boring metals and other materials, in medicine for surgery, in communications, scientific research and holography. They are an integral part of such familiar devices as bar-code scanners used in supermarkets, scanners, laser printers, and compact disc players.

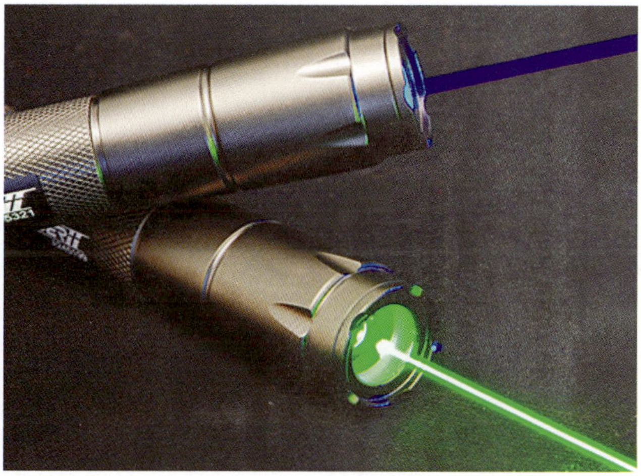



**BITS OF FACT**

A laser printer is a common type of computer printer that rapidly produces high-quality text and graphics on plain paper.

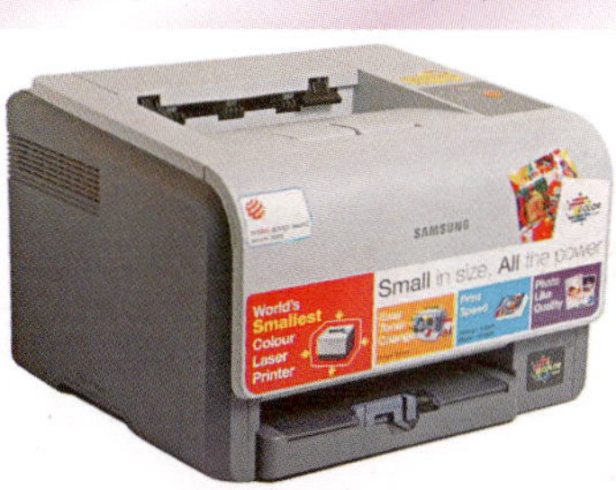

# What is MRI?

MRI stands for Magnetic Resonance Imaging. MRI is a way of getting the pictures of the various parts of your body. To perform an MRI scan, the patient is securely placed on an imaging table within a large MRI scanner. Powerful magnetic fields are administered to align the nuclei within the atoms of the patient's body. Next, radio frequency pulses are applied; finally, the nuclei release some of the radio frequency energy and these emissions are detected by the MRI equipment. With this data, a computer generates a surprisingly detailed view of tissues within the body. The pictures of almost any part of your body can be obtained at almost any particular angle. In particular, the brain, the spinal cord and the nerves are seen much more clearly with MRI than with regular x-rays and CAT scans. Also, muscles, ligaments and tendons are seen quite well. This method of scanning was developed primarily for use in medicine but it has also been used to study fossils and historical artefacts.

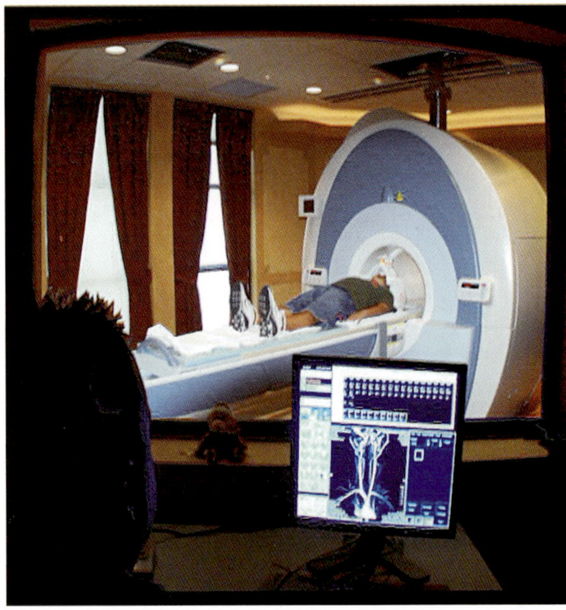

**BITS OF FACT**

X-rays are most often used to detect bone or joint problems or to check the heart and lungs.

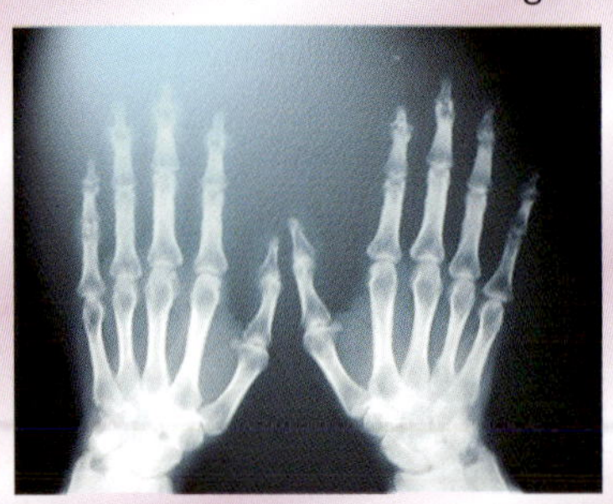

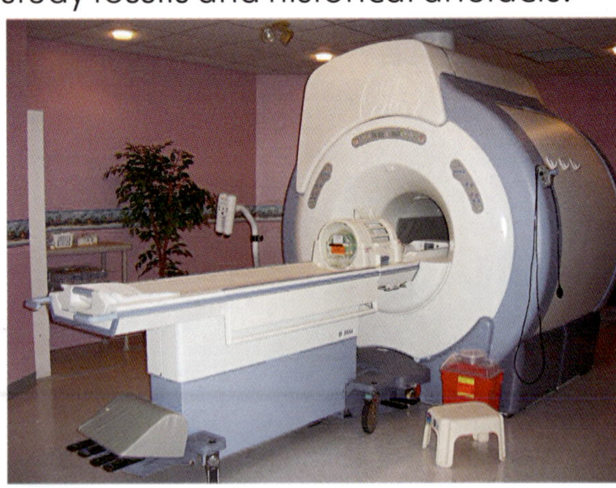

# WHAT IS A KALEIDOSCOPE?

A kaleidoscope resembles a short telescope with a rotating end-piece. When you look through a kaleidoscope, you will see a colourful, geometric pattern. Twisting the end-piece creates ever-changing, mesmerizing new patterns. A kaleidoscope consists of two or more mirrors laid lengthwise inside a tube. Coloured beads, liquid-filled

ampules or other small objects reside in the larger end of the tube. The viewer looks in one end and light enters the other end, reflecting off the mirrors. Typically, there are two rectangular lengthways mirrors. Setting of the mirrors at 45° creates eight duplicate images of the objects, six at 60° and four at 90°. As the tube is rotated, the tumbling of the coloured objects presents the viewer with varying colours and patterns. Any arbitrary pattern of objects shows up as a beautiful symmetric pattern because of the reflections in the mirrors.

Some sources claim that the kaleidoscope was known to ancient Greece, but the Scottish inventor, David Brewster, is credited with its modern invention in 1816.

## BITS OF FACT

A prism is a transparent optical element with flat, polished surfaces that refract light.

# What is a silicon chip?

A silicon chip is an electronic equipment consisting of a small crystal of a silicon semiconductor fabricated to carry out a number of electronic functions in an integrated circuit. A silicon chip is usually less than one centimetre square and about half a millimetre thick. It contains millions of transistors (devices that control the flow of electric current) and other tiny electronic circuit components, packed and interconnected in layers beneath the surface. There is a grid of thin metallic wires on the surface of the chip, which is used to make electrical connections to other devices. This tiny component is responsible for arithmetic, logic, and memory functions in a computer. In addition to being used in computers, silicon chips are used in calculators, microwave ovens, automobile radios and engine controllers, and video cassette recorders (VCRs). The silicon chip was invented in 1961 by two American electrical engineers, Jack Kilby and Robert Noyce.

## BITS OF FACT

A DVD is much like a CD except that it can hold more data. A CD holds about 640MB of data, whereas a single-sided single-layer DVD can hold 4.7GB.

# What is a hovercraft?

A hovercraft is a vehicle that travels above the surface – land or water. A hovercraft has a powerful cushion of downwardly directed air powered by fans and trapped inside a flexible skirt, which greatly increases its lift capacity. A thrust propeller allows the craft to move forwards. The hovercraft was invented in 1952 by Sir Christopher Cockerell, who conducted a simple experiment to prove the principle that a vehicle suspended on a cushion of air would increase the mobility of the vehicle and allow it to traverse a wider variety of terrains.

Modern hovercraft are used for many applications where people or equipment need to travel at speed over water. The hovercraft engine provides the power to drive large fans that blow air under the craft. The air is retained by a rubber 'skirt' that enables the craft to travel over a wide range of terrain. The skirt simply gives way when an obstacle is encountered. The engine also supplies power to a thrust propeller of some kind that pushes the craft forwards on its 'bubble' of air. Rudders, like on an aeroplane, steer the direction of the craft.

**BITS OF FACT**

A sailboat uses the wind as its primary means of propulsion.

# WHAT ARE THE USES OF QUARTZ?

Quartz is a very hard substance – harder than a steel file. Also, most quartz does not split easily. Glass can't transmit ultraviolet light, but quartz can. Quartz is piezoelectric meaning that when an electrical current passes throught it, it vibrates a little bit. When put under pressure, quartz can generate a small electric charge by itself. Quartz is commonly used in the industrial world for various purposes, such as for making special lenses, prisms and quartz-glass tubes for lamps. Quartz is also used in the manufacturing of the tubes, crucibles and glass which are used in a laboratory. Quartz has diverse applications such as its use in an ordinary glass-manufacturing factory for making glass, as a material used in the construction business and in the foundry industry for making moulds. It is also used as a filter for some liquids, in the manufacturing of sandpaper and whetstones, in the scouring of powders, in sandblasting. Quartz digital watches are known the world over for their precision.

## BITS OF FACT

Besides the industrial uses, v can be used as jewellery and for other gem purposes.

# WHAT IS A BLAST FURNACE?

Blast furnaces are usually tall shaft-type steel vessels, up to ten storeys high, internally lined with refractory brick and superimposed over a crucible-like hearth. The purpose of a blast furnace is to reduce chemically and convert iron oxides physically into liquid iron called hot metal or pig iron. The necessary charge to produce molten pig iron consists of iron-bearing materials, coke and flux. The charge is introduced into the furnace at the top. Blasts of heated air from large blast stoves, and in most cases gaseous, liquid, or powdered fuel, are injected into the furnace through openings at the bottom of the shaft just above the hearth crucible. As the hot air encounters the coke, the coke is burned along with the injected fuels, producing the necessary heat and reducing gas to remove oxygen from the ore in the reduction process. As the iron melts, it descends and accumulates in the crucible. The molten pig iron and slag are drained from the crucible through different tapping holes. The gas that exits from the top of the furnace goes through a cleaning process.

**BITS OF FACT**

Iron is one of the most widespread elements on the Earth. It makes up approximately 5 per cent of the Earth's crust.

# WHAT IS LPG?

LPG is Liquefied Petroleum Gas. Liquefied Petroleum Gases (LPG) are obtained by the refining of crude oil and from natural gas by oil absorption or refrigerated absorption process. LP Gases are mixtures of hydrocarbons, which are gaseous at normal ambient temperature and atmospheric pressure, but can be liquefied at normal ambient temperature by the application of moderate pressure. LPG is stored and transported in containers as a liquid, but is generally drawn out and used as a gas. LPG in gaseous state is nearly twice as heavy as air. Liquid LPG is almost half as heavy as water. When liquid LPG gets converted to a gaseous state, it expands by about 250 times. LPG can be used for various applications such as– (a) Household - Cooking/ Heating / Lighting (b) Agriculture - Grain drying / Weed killing / Preservation of fruits / tobacco curing / Tea drying (c) Automobile - Heat treatment / Paint baking (d) Ceramics - Biscuit & Glost firing of porcelain & stoneware (e) Chemicals & Drugs - Heating & Drying (f) Electrical - Bulbs & Tubelights manufacture / filament manufacture/Battery.

**BITS OF FACT**

Thomas Ahearn invented the electric cooking range in 1892 and installed one in the Windsor Hotel in Montreal.

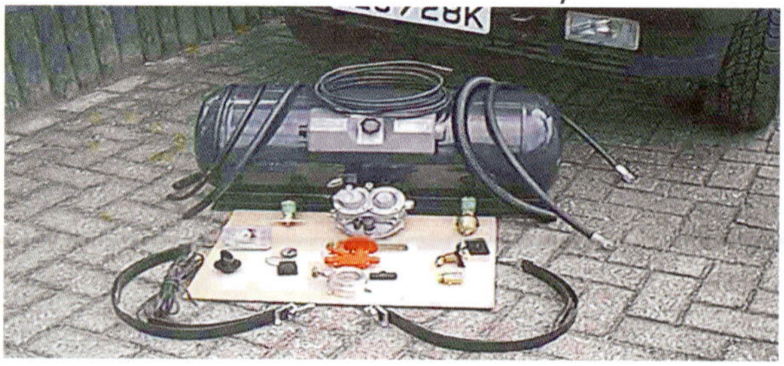

# WHAT IS A SUNDIAL?

A sundial is essentially a clock. But more specifically, it is a clock that uses the position of the sun to indicate the time. A sundial is the most primitive form of a clock. The simplest sundial consists of a stick set in the ground, which casts a shadow indicating the time of day. No one can be sure when the first sundial appeared. But we do know that as early as 3500 B.C., the Egyptians were building sundials that not only kept time but also indicated the longest and shortest day of the year. We have days and nights on the Earth as the Earth rotates around its axis. Approximately, every 23.6 hours, our Earth makes one complete rotation and as we rotate, we rotate away from the sun (night) and back towards it (day). A sundial works by gauging the sun's position in the sky relative to where we are in that 24-hour period. The sun casts shadows on the sundial in different places as it moves across our sky, indicating different times. The time piece on the sundial is called a "gnomon". By reading where the shadow falls when the sun hits the gnomon, we can estimate the time of day.

**BITS OF FACT**

The Giant Sundial of Jantar Mantar in Jaipur, India, is the largest sundial in the world, standing 27m tall.

# WHAT GOES FASTER, BULLETS OR ROCKETS?

A bullet is a solid projectile propelled by a firearm or air gun and is normally made from metal (usually lead). A rocket is a vehicle, missile or aircraft which obtains thrust by the reaction to the ejection of fast moving fluid from within a rocket engine. Rockets go about 25 times faster than the fastest bullets. If a bullet went as fast as a rocket, it would escape the Earth's gravity and keep going perhaps to Mars. Indeed, the Earth's escape velocity (ignoring air friction) is almost 10 times the fastest bullet 25,000 mph (40,320 km/h). In 2001, the spacecraft Odyssey left the Earth for Mars at about 67,100 mph (1,08,000 km/h) and cruised thereafter at about 54,000 mph (87,000 km/h). The fastest bullet (probably the Winchester .223 Super Short Magnum) has a muzzle velocity of about 4,000 feet per second or 2,700 mph (4,400 km/h).

**BITS OF FACT**

The father of modern rocket propulsion is an American whose name is Dr Robert Hutchings Goddard. By 1926, Goddard had constructed and tested successfully the first rocket using liquid fuel. Indeed, the flight of Goddard's rocket on 16th March, 1926, at Auburn, Massachusetts, was a great achievement in history.

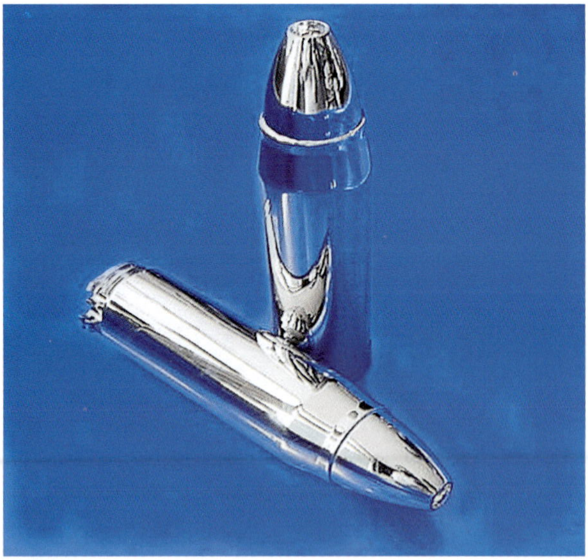

# WHAT ARE GERMS?

Germs are tiny organisms or living things that can cause disease. Germs are so small and sneaky that they creep into our bodies without being noticed. In fact, germs are so tiny that you need to use a microscope to see them. Once germs have invaded our bodies, they snuggle in for a long stay. They gobble up nutrients and energy, and can produce toxins, which are like poisons. Those toxins can cause the

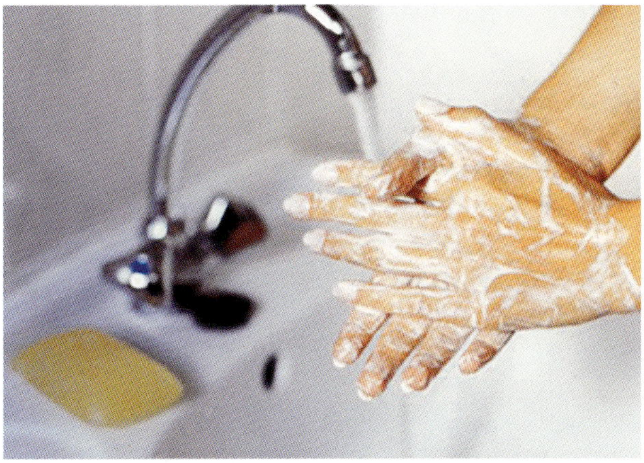

symptoms of common infections, like fevers, sniffles, rashes, coughing, vomiting, and diarrhoea. Germs spread through the air when someone coughs or sneezes. Germs can also appear in bodily fluids like saliva, sweat and blood. The best way to avoid getting germs is to stay away from these areas where germs spread. There are many different kinds of germs, but the four most common are: bacteria, viruses, fungi and protozoa. Each of these types of germs causes different symptoms or illnesses. For instance, while bacteria germs cause minor illnesses such as ear infections, sore throats and cavities, viruses cause more serious diseases such as chicken pox, measles and the flu.

## BITS OF FACT

Protozoa are single-celled organisms that love moisture and often spread diseases through water. Some protozoa cause intestinal infections that lead to diarrhoea, nausea and belly pain.

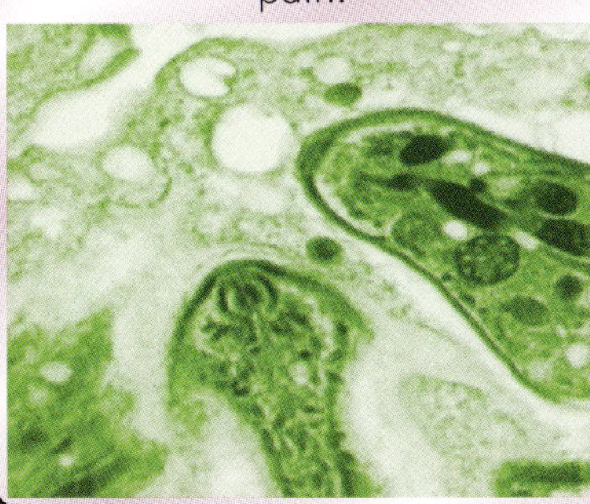

# What is quicksand?

Quicksand is not a unique type of soil; it is usually just sand or another type of grainy soil. Quicksand is nothing more than a soupy mixture of sand and water. Quicksand is just ordinary sand, but it can cause one to sink because it becomes oversaturated with water and the friction between sand particles is reduced. The resulting sand is a mushy mixture of sand and water that can no longer support any weight. Sand slips apart rapidly when weight is put onto it, as a person stepping on it might do. Hence, the term quicksand applies to sand that quickly allows one to sink into it. People tend to be drowned in quicksand if they flail their arms and legs about. This makes them sink because they are literally helping the quicksand split apart. On the other hand, the person who does not panic and who puts one's hands and legs slightly apart, moving as slowly as possible, will not sink under the quicksand.

**BITS OF FACT**

If sand contains a lot of silica, it can be melted down into glass with high heat. Do you know glass beads were being created and used well before the Roman Empire stood.

# WHAT IS A MAGNETIC COMPASS?

A compass is an extremely simple device. A magnetic compass consists of a small, lightweight magnet balanced on a nearly frictionless pivot point. The magnet is generally called a needle. One

end of the needle is often marked "N," for north. The magnetic compass is an old Chinese invention, probably first made in China during the Qin dynasty (221-206 B.C.). It is the oldest instrument for navigation and has been a vital tool for navigators at sea for centuries. The compass allows a ship to steer a selected course. A magnetic compass works because the Earth is like a giant magnet, surrounded by a huge magnetic field. The Earth has two magnetic poles which lie near the North and South poles. The magnetic field of the Earth causes a magnetized 'needle' of iron or steel to swing into a north-south position if it is hung from a thread or if it is stuck through a straw or piece of wood floating in a bowl of water. Needles were magnetized by stroking them with lodestones, lumps of magnetic rocks called magnetites.

## BITS OF FACT

The first person recorded to have used the compass as a navigational aid was Zheng. He (1371-1435) was from the Yunnan province in China. He made seven ocean voyages between 1405 and 1433.

# What is the history of dynamite?

Dynamite is one example of a chemical explosive. An explosive is anything that, once ignited, burns very rapidly and produces a large amount of hot gas in the process. The hot gas expands very quickly and applies pressure. A Swedish industrialist, engineer and inventor, Alfred Nobel, built bridges and buildings in Stockholm. His construction work inspired Nobel to research new methods of blasting rocks. In 1860, Alfred first started experimenting with nitroglycerine. Nitroglycerine was first invented by an Italian chemist, Ascanio Sobrero, in 1846. In its natural liquid state, nitroglycerine is very volatile. Alfred Nobel understood this. In 1866, he discovered that mixing nitroglycerine with silica would turn the liquid into a malleable paste, called dynamite. One advantage of dynamite over nitroglycerine was that it could be cylinder-shaped for insertion into the drilling holes used for mining.

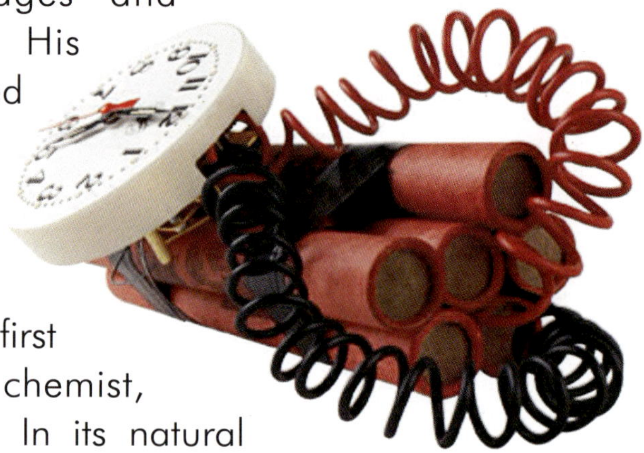

**BITS OF FACT**

The first fireworks were probably made in China, about 2,000 years ago.

# What is the Thames Barrier?

The Thames Barrier has been described as the eighth wonder of the world. It is certainly a very impressive work of engineering. London was often subjected to flooding in the past. The main possible cause of flooding in London area is surge tides. These originate in the North Atlantic, and generally pass to the north of the British Isles. Occasionally, northerly winds force them down into the North Sea, sending millions of tons of extra water up River Thames. In 1953, floods occurred, during which over 300 people were drowned and 160,000 acres of farmland were flooded with salt water. Several schemes were proposed and rejected. In 1965, a barrier was proposed to be built. The 1,716 feet width of the river is divided by nine reinforced concrete piers to form six openings for shipping and four other openings. The piers are founded on solid chalk, over 50 feet below the level of the river. The four largest steel gates are 200 feet wide and weigh 1,500 tonnes each. In addition, eleven and a half miles of the river, to the east of the barrier, was protected by new walls, to a new defence level of 23 feet.

**BITS OF FACT**

St Paul's Cathedral is a cathedral on Ludgate Hill in the city of London. It is the seat of the Bishop of London.

# What is a glider?

A glider is an unpowered aircraft, *i.e.* an aeroplane without a motor. Gliders along with most other aircraft are designed to have skins that are as smooth as possible to allow the planes to slip more easily through the air. Early gliders were constructed from wood covered with canvas. Later, aluminium was used but it decreased the performance of the glider. In many modern gliders, composite construction using materials such as fiberglass and carbon fibre are quickly replacing aluminium. A glider has only three main forces acting on it: lift, drag and weight. For a glider to fly, it must generate lift to oppose its weight. Stet lift, a glider must move through the air. But the motion of a glider through the air also generates drag. In a powered aircraft, the thrust from the engine opposes drag. But a glider has no engine to generate thrust. With the drag unopposed, a glider quickly slows down until it can no longer generate enough lift to oppose the weight.

**BITS OF FACT**

Helicopters are safest to fly in bad weather because they can slow down, stop and/or fly backwards or sideways.

# WHAT IS A BOOMERANG?

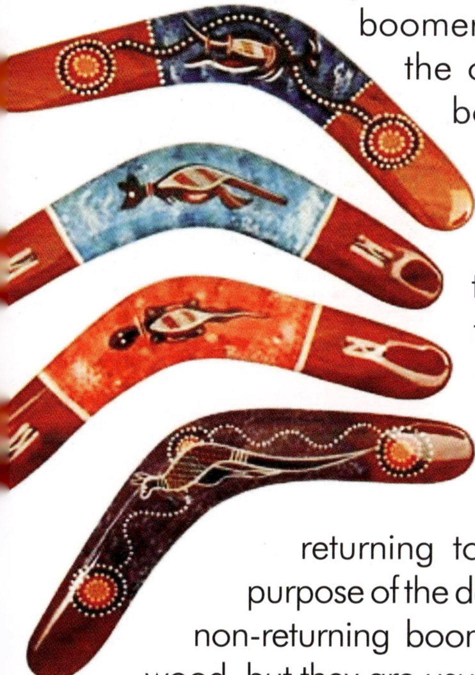

A boomerang, also known as a throwing stick, is a wooden item often shaped in the form of an open flat V or a cross. A boomerang can also take other forms, but only the open V and the X formats are returning boomerangs. A non-returning boomerang was used mostly by Australian aborigines as a hunting weapon or even as a replacement for fighting sticks. When thrown correctly, a returning boomerang flies through the air in a circular path and arrives back at its starting point. Returning boomerangs are not suited for hunting as they are very hard to aim at. Actually, hitting a target would stop it from returning to the thrower, pretty much defeating the purpose of the design. Returning boomerangs evolved out of non-returning boomerangs. These are also curved pieces of wood, but they are usually heavier and longer, typically 1 metre or more across. A non-returning boomerang does not have the light weight and special wing design that causes a returning boomerang to travel back to the thrower, but its curved shape does cause it to fly easily through the air.

**BITS OF FACT**

The yo-yo has enjoyed many periods of popularity throughout world history and may be the second oldest toy in the world (after dolls).

# WHAT IS GLUE?

Glue is a compound that sticks or bonds two items together. Glue is made from natural sources or synthetically. Early glues were animal glues made by blending animal products like the use of buffalo hooves. The first glues were natural gums and other plant resins or saps. It was believed that the Sumerian people were the first to use it until it was discovered that Neanderthals, as far back as 50,000 years, made adhesives from birch bark. The Egyptians used animal glues to adhere tombs, furniture, ivory and papyrus. Today, there are four main types of glues – Natural Glues: These are based on natural resin (from vegetables) or from animal skins. Synthetic Glues: Glues like thermo-setting glues are synthetic glues. Hot Glues: Applied hot and allowed to harden as they cool. These adhesives have become popular for crafts because of their ease of use. Reactive Glues: Glues that react with the surface they are sticking to. They are often used to reduce the loosening of bolts and screws.

**BITS OF FACT**

The natural gums include agar, from colloids in marine plants, algin that is derived from seaweed, and gum arabic, an extract of the acacia tree (also known as the gum tree).

# What is clay and what are its uses?

Clay is a common name for a number of fine-grained, earthy materials that become plastic when wet. Chemically, clays are hydrous aluminium silicates, ordinarily containing impurities, e.g., potassium, sodium, calcium, magnesium or iron in small amounts. Clays often form colloidal suspensions when immersed in water, but the clay particles flocculate (clump) and settle quickly in saline water. Clays are easily moulded into a form that they retain when dry. They become hard and lose their plasticity when subjected to heat. Since prehistoric times, clay has been indispensable in architecture, in industry and in agriculture. As a building material, it is used in the form of brick, either sun-dried (adobe) or fired. Clays are also of great industrial importance, e.g., in the manufacture of tiles for wall and floor coverings, of porcelain, china and earthenware, and of pipes for drainage and sewage.

## BITS OF FACT

China Clay is used in wide varieties of paints like distemper, cement primer, wood primer, emulsion paint, texture coating, spray plaster, putties, fillers and undercoats.

# WHAT IS YEAST AND HOW DOES IT WORK?

Yeast is a tiny plant-like micro-organism that exists all around us – in soil, on plants and even in the air. It is capable of reproducing itself.

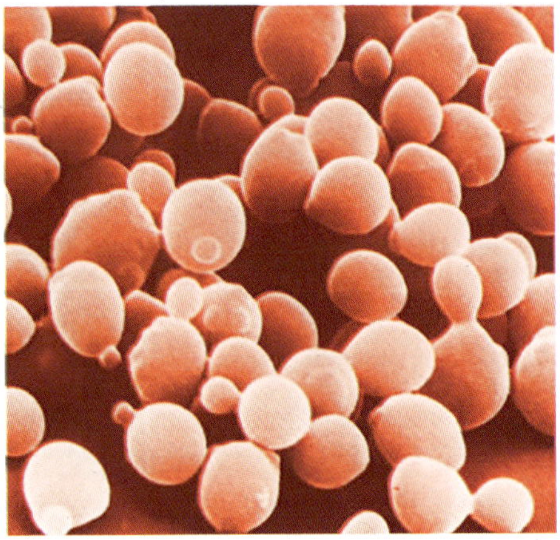

From one tiny yeast cell, tons of yeast can be produced. A piece of yeast consists of minute cells, with walls composed of cellulose, and an interior of living matter called protoplasm. They are mostly used for beer and wine fermentations and bread production. The main purpose of yeast is to serve as a catalyst in the process of fermentation, which is essential in the making of bread. It was Louis Pasteur in 1859 who first discovered how yeast works. The little cells we mentioned ferment the dough and produce tiny bubbles of gas inside it. As a result, the dough gets fatter and bigger, and rises. Thus, when the dough is baked, you have a loaf which is light and airy. When you cut it, you can see all the tiny holes formed by the gas, so that it may look like a sponge.

## BITS OF FACT

Wheat is the major ingredient in most breads, rolls, crackers, cookies, biscuits, cakes, doughnuts, muffins, pancakes, waffles, noodles, piecrusts, ice cream cones, macaroni, spaghetti, puddings, pizzas and several other items.

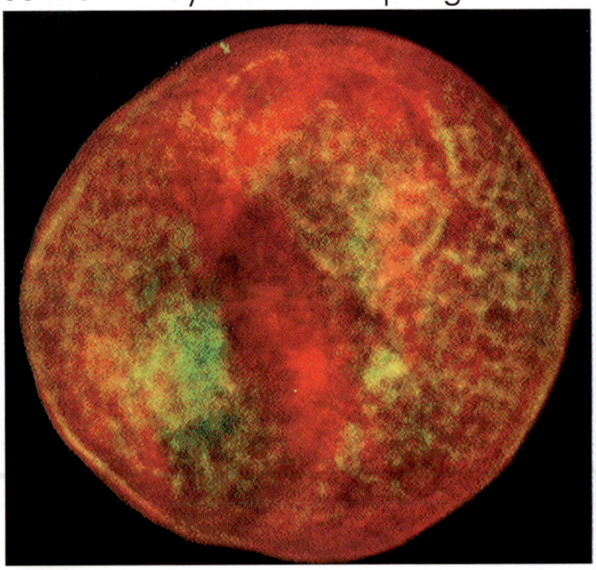

# WHAT IS THE HISTORY OF COFFEE?

Coffee is a widely-consumed stimulant beverage prepared from roasted seeds, commonly called coffee beans of the coffee plant.

Coffee was first consumed in the 9th century when it was discovered in the highlands of Ethiopia. According to one story, the effect of coffee beans on behaviour was noticed by a sheep herder from Caffa Ethiopia. His name was Kaldi as he tended his sheep. He noticed that the sheep became hyperactive after eating the red "cherries" from a certain plant when they changed pastures. He tried a few himself, and was soon as overactive as his herd. Coffee berries, which contain the coffee bean, are produced by several species of small evergreen bush of the genus Coffea. Once ripe, coffee berries are picked, processed and dried. The seeds are, then, roasted, undergoing several physical and chemical changes. They are roasted to varying degrees, depending on the desired flavour. They are, then, ground and brewed to create coffee.

**BITS OF FACT**

Tea contains half the amount of caffeine found in coffee. The number of recommended cups of tea to drink every day is 4. This gives you optimal benefit.

# WHAT IS BALLET?

Ballet is one of the world's most graceful dance styles. Ballet dancing is known for its grace and elegance as ballerinas seem to glide across the stage almost effortlessly. Ballet is a form of dancing performed for theatre audiences. Like other dance forms, ballet may tell a story, express a mood or may reflect the music. A ballet dancer's technique and skills differ a lot from other dancers. Ballet dancers perform many movements that are unnatural. When all of these movements are well executed, they look natural.

Ballet dancers seem to ignore the laws of gravity. They float through the air in long, slow leaps. They keep perfect balance while they spin like tops. During certain steps, their feet move so rapidly that the eye can hardly follow. Female dancers raise themselves even higher by going up on their toes with pointe shoes. Pointe shoes make it possible for ballerinas to dance on the tips of their toes.

**BITS OF FACT**

In Bharatanatyam, Kathak and Odissi, dancers wear heavy anklets of multiple bells called ghungroos. Ghungroos highlight and emphasize the rhythms of the dancers' feet.

# What is an igloo and how is it made?

The igloo is a temporary winter hunting shelter for the Alaskan Eskimo. An igloo is shaped like a dome with a tunnel entrance to trap cold air. It is made of hard blocks of snow. First the fresh snow is cut into blocks. Then, the blocks are laid on their edges to form a circle and the end result is a narrowing spiral. The igloo is blocked with edges cut wider above than below, into the remaining gap in the roof. The gaps between the blocks of snow are covered with additional snow. Then, the Eskimo enters the igloo with a whale blubber lamp. The lamp is lighted to the highest possible setting and the entrance is blocked with a block of ice. Inside the igloo, the snow on the roof begins to melt. Because of its domed design, the water melts down the sides of the igloo and soaks the blocks of snow. When the blocks are almost completely saturated with water, the Eskimo allows the frigid outside air to rush in, transforming the fragile snow structure into one of hard, solid ice.

**BITS OF FACT**

The skin canoe, known as a kayak, is one of the most highly manoeuvrable small craft used by the Eskimos.

# What is a valley?

A valley is an area of elongated lowland, surrounded by much higher hills or mountains. Valleys are formed in a number of ways. A rift valley is formed through the separation of the Earth's crust, caused by violent tectonic movements; a notable example of a rift valley is the Great Rift Valley in Africa. River valleys are formed through the slow process of erosion over the course of centuries. They typically have a V-shaped profile. Valleys that are not V-shaped were formerly occupied by glaciers and are characteristically U-shaped, formed by the huge bodies of ice that moved along; they carved the valleys as they passed, carrying away giant boulders and huge amounts of debris. Narrow deep valleys are sometimes called canyons. Valleys usually have rich deposits of alluvial mud, making them ideal for agriculture. As a result, many human civilizations have settled in valleys, taking advantage of the rivers, which often wind through valleys, as sources of water.

## BITS OF FACT

The Grand Canyon cuts through the Colorado Plateau that is between 5,000 and 9,000 feet above the sea level. It is 277 miles long, up to 18 miles wide and 5,000 feet deep.

# What is a Tattoo and What Makes it So Long-Lasting?

A tattoo is a puncture wound, made deep in your skin, that's filled with ink. It's made by penetrating your skin with a needle and injecting ink into the area, usually creating some sort of design. What makes tattoos so long-lasting is that they're so deep that the ink isn't injected into the epidermis (the top layer of skin that you continue to produce and shed throughout your lifetime). Instead, the ink is injected into the dermis, which is the second deeper layer of skin. Dermis cells are very stable. So, the tattoo is practically permanent.

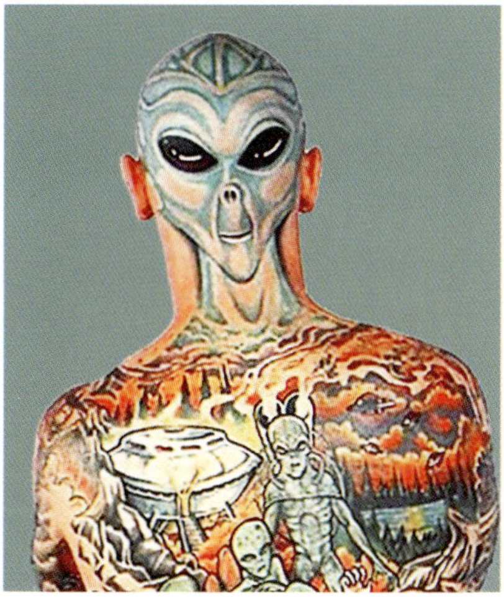

Tattoos used to be done manually, that is the tattoo artist would puncture the skin with a needle and inject the ink by hand. Though this process is still used in some parts of the world yet most tattoo shops use tattoo machines these days. A tattoo machine is a handheld electric instrument that uses a tube and needle system. On one end is a sterilized needle, which is attached to tubes that contain ink. A foot switch is used to turn on the machine, which moves the needle in and out while driving the ink about 1/8 inch into your skin.

**BITS OF FACT**

Mehandi is the name of the ancient art of painting patterns on the body with henna paste, and the resulting stains left on the skin.

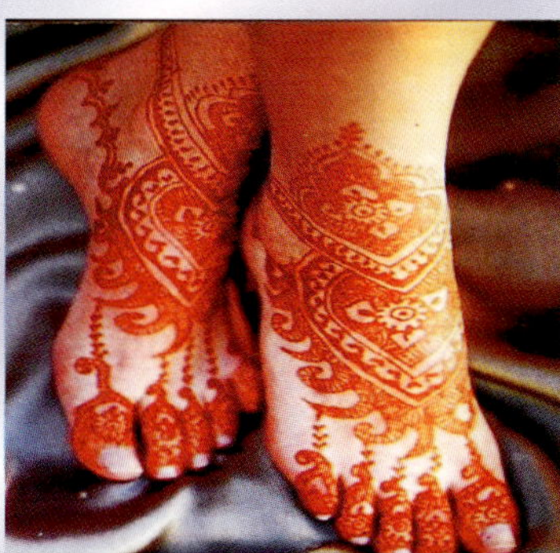

# WHAT ARE THE ADVANTAGES OF SMS?

SMS is an acronym standing for Short Message Service. It lets you send short text and numeric messages to and from digital cell phones, cell phones and e-mail addresses, as well as cell phones and public SMS messaging gateways on the Internet. SMS is convenient and cost-effective for a number of reasons. When you compare it with the cost of airtime for voice calls or wireless web access, SMS is a real bargain. Messages can be received while making voice calls. There are no busy signals to contend with. In addition to this, if you find yourself in a situation where talking on a cell phone is inappropriate, SMS is silent and discreet. Messages generated by SMS are immediately delivered directly to your phone. There is no need to call an access number, as is the case with voice-mail. A single short message can be up to 160 characters of text in length. Those 160 characters can consist of words or numbers or an alphanumeric combination.

## BITS OF FACT

Several modern ways of sending messages have come into use due to which people have almost forgotten to write letters by hand.

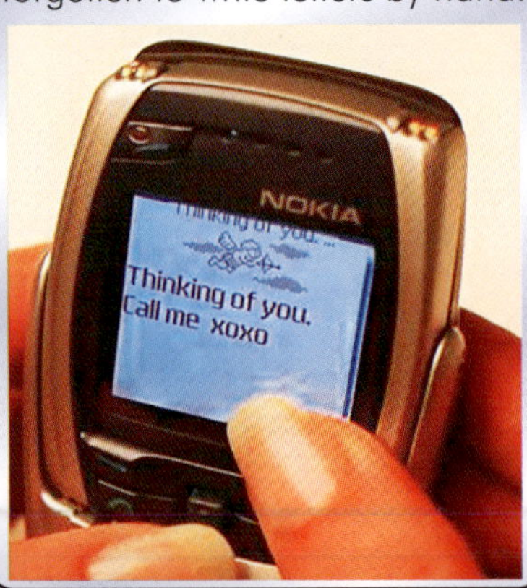

# What are the birds of prey?

The birds that feed on other animals are called the birds of prey. Some of the most common predators are eagles, hawks, vultures, falcons, kestrels and buzzards. Most birds of prey are strong fliers with sharp eyes, hooked beaks and powerful talons or claws. They kill their prey with their strong, sharp claws and, then, pull and tear the flesh with their narrow, hooked beaks. These birds usually swallow large chunks of food. The birds of prey attack in several ways. The kestrel hunts by hovering over an open ground and, then, pouncing upon its prey before it can escape. Birds of prey have a very good eyesight. As they hover many metres above the ground, they can detect the slightest movement of a mouse in the grass below. The falcon stoops or dives its head first at its prey and catches it in its claws. Vultures are the biggest birds of prey. They do not hunt. Rather, they feed on carrion (dead animals). The peregrine falcon while stooping on its prey can reach speeds of 350 km/hr.

**BITS OF FACT**

The palmnut vulture is the only vegetarian bird of prey and it feeds on oil nuts.

# What were the first shoes made of?

Scientists estimate people first wore animal skins during the Ice Age (5 million years ago). Rough shoes protected the feet of Stone Age people from rocks and thorns. The first suggestion of foot coverings appeared in rock paintings from the late Palaeolithic period (15,000 years ago). Early man, in warmer climates, invented the sandal to protect his feet from sharp rocks. He did so by strapping a mat of woven grass, a strip of animal hide or a slab of flat wood to his feet with "thongs" he cut out of the animal-hide. Spanish cave paintings show humans with animal skins around their feet. In Ancient Egypt, sandals were made from papyrus and palm leaves. The first rubber soled shoes, called plimsolls, were developed and manufactured in the United States in the late 1800s. Wealthy ancient Egyptians wore sandals as long as 5,000 years ago, and designed different shoes for different purposes.

## BITS OF FACT

An alligator-skin is an exotic leather made from the belly-skin of an alligator. This is top-quality leather that is commonly used for shoes, gun cases, purses, wallets and belts.

# What are the different kinds of whales?

There are about 80 species of whales. Although they live in the sea yet they are not fish but mammals. They are warm-blooded and give birth

to young ones which feed on their mothers' milk. There are two types of whales – the whale-bone or baleeen whales and the toothed whales. Baleen whales have a comb of thin plates, called baleen, instead of teeth. They feed on plankton, which are made up of tiny sea creatures and plants. The whales strain plankton from the water by sieving them through their baleens which hang from their top jaws. Baleen whales include blue whales, right whales, humpback whales and grey whales. Most toothed whales are smaller than baleen whales. Toothed whales have teeth and prey on large fish and seals. Toothed whales include killer whales, sperm whales, porpoises and dolphins. The black and white killer whale is the most dangerous of all the whales.

### BITS OF FACT

The blue whale is the largest creature of the world. It can grow to a length of 30 m and can weigh more than 150 tonnes.

# WHAT IS BALSA?

Balsa is the lightest and softest commercially sold wood in the world. Balsa wood is used in many applications that require high levels of floatation, life-saving equipment, floats, rafts etc. as well as insulation and in sound absorption applications. It is also used in model aircraft building and in architectural /engineering models of many sorts. In fact, it is used in any type of model building where it is important to have a wood that is light and/or easily cut and shaped with hand tools. The secret to the lightness of balsa wood can only be seen with a microscope. The cells are big and very thin-walled so that the ratio of solid matter to open space may be as small as possible. Most of the wood has the gobs of heavy, plastic-like cement, called lignin, holding the cells together. In balsa, lignin is at a minimum. Only about 40% of the volume of a piece of balsa is solid substance. Green balsa wood typically contains five times as much water by weight as it has actual wood substance, compared to other hardwood which contains very little water in relation to wood substance.

**BITS OF FACT**

The heaviest and hardest wood in the world is Snakewood. It is used for umbrella handles, walking sticks, caskets, fancy items, cabinets.

# What is the history of the band-aid?

Earle Dickson was employed as a cotton buyer for the Johnson & Johnson when he invented the band-aid in 1921. His wife Josephine Dickson was always cutting her fingers in the kitchen while preparing food. At that time, a bandage consisted of separate gauze and adhesive tape was available. Earle Dickson noticed that the gauze and adhesive tape she used would soon fall off her active fingers. He decided to invent something that would stay in place and protect small wounds better. He sat down with some tape and gauze and a pair of scissors. Then, he cut the tape into strips. In the middle of each strip, he stuck a little square of gauze and, then, covered the product with crinoline to keep it sterile. Since then, whenever Josephine had an accident, ready-made bandages were there for her to use quickly. At Johnson & Johnson, they heard about these new bandages that could be put on in thirty seconds. Since that day, band-aids came into use on a wide scale.

## BITS OF FACT

Dettol is a proven safe and effective concentrated antiseptic disinfectant, that kills bacteria and provides expert protection against the germs which can cause infection and illness.

# What are the dimensions of the Eiffel Tower?

The Eiffel Tower is located on the Left Bank of River Seine in Paris. The tower is 324 metres tall today, which is about 108 storeys. Originally, it had no television tower. So, it was 12 metres shorter. The levels accessible to the public are at heights of 57.63 metres or 19 storeys; 115.73 metres or 38 storeys; and 273 metres or 89 storeys. The base of the tower covers a square area of 100 metres (the length of an American football field) on a side. The tower weighs 7,300 metric tons. The tower was built by the engineering firm of Gustave Eiffel, Eiffel et Cie, a company well established in metallic construction projects. The Eiffel Tower is built of pure iron. Eiffel built it of puddled iron, a type of traditional wrought iron, prepared in a special way in a special furnace so that the iron may be made very pure and strong. Construction was started on 26th January 1887 and was completed on 31th March 1889. So, it took two years, two months and five days to build this tower. The tower was built as the "theme structure" of the Universal Exposition of 1889, which was held in Paris.

**BITS OF FACT**

The Golden Gate Bridge is a suspension bridge spanning the Golden Gate, the opening of the San Francisco Bay onto the Pacific Ocean.